Reformation of
the Heart, Soul and Mind

by C. Matthew McMahon

Copyright Information

Table of Contents

Introduction

How many Christians and ministers have you met who are sowing reformation in their churches in tears? Or for that matter, how many preachers have truly preached in such a way as to set their people on fire through the unction and power of the Spirit of God and his word to reap something before God that is spiritually beneficial, heartily reformed yet laced with Christian joy? Where are all those people who should be *pressing into the Kingdom? Striving* to enter at the straight gate? Do we see this in our day in all our churches? Or is it difficult to see?

When you sit to reflect on the state of the contemporary church all around the globe in our day, it is a matter of sadness and of utmost importance for prayer. In the hundreds of thousands of churches, maybe millions, across the land, there is not a single united Scriptural ripple that is changing the face of the people of God for true biblical reformation. Why is that? I think you will be surprised at my answer. I think you will be surprised at the answer *Scripture* gives. I think you will be surprised at what *Jesus* says about this. And when we ponder, in this study, what that answer actually is, and when we understand it, we will have a far better strategy for our own lives, and for prayer, to see biblical reformation take place in the world for the glory of King Jesus.

All Christians around the world need true biblical and spiritual reformation. But the manner in which that reformation takes place is housed directly in the fundamentals of the Christian religion: key concepts that are tied to biblical reform that stem from the teaching of the Bible. Where are the great awakenings? Where are the new "reformations" of religion in the church? Where is the revival that takes us *back to the sources* of the bible and to the fundamentals of Christianity that we would exercise ourselves in love, and see spiritual growth in the church? The church today will never see another Great Awakening until they *get their spiritual act together,* and that quickly – take a look around, God has already sent a worldwide coronavirus to the church, and the church has done ... what ... with it? Ignored it? Hoped things would get better quickly so they could get back to doing what they did before? Can a worldwide pandemic be a means to spark reform? We will have to see how that works out in the life of the church, but it isn't looking too good a year and a half into it this far.

If the word of God is the only rule for faith and practice in the church where Jesus Christ is Head, then it is the only place, the only means, harnessed by the Sovereign Spirit of Christ, where true biblical reformation according to God's prescription can "be done." Reformation is to be found *there.* But what *constitutes* reform? What do Christians need to do to see reform? Should they, as at Pentecost, just *wait*

5

around for tongues of fire to pop out of the air and land on their head again? Or is there something the Spirit of God requires them to do?

In this study, we will consider how reformation is linked to Jesus' universal and perpetual teaching of loving God and loving one's neighbor, as it pertains to the heart, soul and mind. Such a biblical reformation of the heart, soul and mind, and considering it, presses us to reflect whether we do what Christ commands of his people, or not. Are we listening to him, and do we desire biblical reformation as it pertains to his godly will? Or is reformation just something we fantasize about in historical books on the magisterial reformation? The home (which is a little church), the church itself, the workplace, the state, the country you live in; in fact, all of society throughout the world for the glory of the great King, Jesus Christ, and the Kingdom of God, must be set under God's words, Christ's words, and strive for a continued spiritual reform for the glory of the Redeemer. And what is the *motivating* factor in all this for reformation? What does the Spirit use to reform people?

The *love* that Christians ought to have in light of biblical reformation, consist in loving God with *all* the heart, soul and mind, *and* loving one's neighbor. That is a nice sentiment, and it is the teaching of Scripture, (see Matthew 22), but at this point, you may have no idea *how* that plays out, or what is required of you to actually accomplish such a task. You think about it like the world thinks about it, it's the golden rule. Be kind to people, and do good to them, the way you would like them to be good to you. And, oh yes, love God too. You are just thinking about *winging* it at this point. "Love God" means to you whatever you want it to mean, and "love your neighbor" means to you that you should be nice to people. But really, is that what *Jesus* meant? Where did he get such a notion, and what was he teaching?

Love to God with inflamed spiritual affections, *all* of them, in every part, all the time, to the highest degree of holiness, by the power of the Spirit, to walk victoriously in abundant life as a daily occurrence, is what he was teaching, (1 Corinthians 16:12; Ephesians 6:24; Philippians 3:9). You see there, once we start talking in that way, you dismiss the idea as too high and lofty. You have *already* dismissed the idea as something *impossible* to obtain; "loving God" with *all* your heart, soul and mind is impossible for fallen people. To be reformed and changed into his image in this way of "love" is somewhat of an ethereal idea to you at this point. It's an *airy feeling* that has little substance to it though you might have heard it a million times. It is a *generality.* But what if I were to tell you that the very core of biblical reformation is set inside this "love" and that without it, no one can ever be reformed, and no revival will ever take place in the whole world without it? And what if I were to tell you that Jesus was teaching and Old Testament concept, from the Scriptures, which gives a road map to biblical reformation? To people who are Christians, this consideration would be a very important statement or assertion to contemplate. And this assertion is not only going to be scripturally proven, but this is the very task to be demonstrated and covered in this work so that biblical reformation can, at the very least, get started in your life, home, and church.

I will tell you now, and place all the cards on the table here in this introduction. The reformation of the heart, soul and mind is one of the most important, if not *the* most important, spiritual persuasive to loving God that exists in Scripture, and without it, without understanding it aright, there will never be, nor can be, any true reformation of the church. That means whatever "loving God" means, and doing so in the highest degree possible (*all* the heart, soul and mind), to its furthest extent, is the hinge on which all godly reform will occur. It is the tool and means by which the Spirit of God makes people holy, and sanctifies them, without which, reformation is nothing but theory. This is contained in the words of Jesus when he says, "Thou shalt love the Lord thy God with all thy heart, and with all thy soul, and with all thy mind. This is the first and great commandment. And the second is like unto it, Thou shalt love thy neighbour as thyself," (Matt. 22:37-39). Do people do this? Yes, I know, no one can do this. Hold that thought for a time.

Let me press you to consider this question personally: "do you love God with all your heart, soul and mind?" I know that you will answer, "no one does."

Let's cut to the chase now and say, that's the greatest excuse all people have ever given to continue in sin, and to dismiss a godly reformation. You need to throw that sentiment out. God never speaks that way in Scripture to simply dismiss actions by thinking they are too hard, and Christ never teaches anything that way. In fact, the words of Matthew 22:37-39 are *his* words, and *he* said them. You might think, "It is true he said it, but he didn't mean it, really, in that way." That's just another denial that Antinomians use to dismiss godly obedience (You might not know what an Antinomian is, but we will cover that in this work as well). Yes, Jesus did mean what he said. In fact, he meant it to its superlative degree. Seem impossible? How does reformation and loving God fit together? And how is it reformation of the heart, soul and mind *for* God's glory and *our* good? This is the substance of this work, and hopefully, by the end of it, we will have a solid, biblical answer to how reform should take place in the life of every Christian. So, let's get started...

Chapter 1:
Reformation in Light of the Law

"But when the Pharisees had heard that he had put the Sadducees to silence, they were gathered together. Then one of them, which was a lawyer, asked him a question, tempting him, and saying, Master, which is the great commandment in the law? Jesus said unto him, Thou shalt love the Lord thy God with all thy heart, and with all thy soul, and with all thy mind. This is the first and great commandment. And the second is like unto it, Thou shalt love thy neighbour as thyself. On these two commandments hang all the law and the prophets," (Matt. 22:34-40).

What is the greatest commandment God ever gave anyone at any time? This is a very good question for people to ponder. We are not obliged by this question to pick one commandment at the expense of others. The answer is really, "everything God has ever said is commanded to us, and all men are to obey everything God commands in both character and conduct."[1] This idea is really the sum of Jesus' answer to the lawyer who was questioning him. Jesus had silenced the Sadducees on their erroneous and heretical view of the

---

[1] Being a good disciple under the authority of Christ, is to be led by Christ, through the Spirit, to conform to him in character and conduct. See my work, *Walking Victoriously in the Power of the Spirit* for a full discussion of this idea.

resurrection, and the Pharisees liked that he did so. They gathered, then, to pose certain questions to Jesus. They were always trying to trap him and discredit him. One of them, a scribe, a lawyer, in which the Gospel writer uses such a term to set forth a person who knows the law well by way of knowledge, tests Jesus asking him a question. "Teacher, which is the great commandment in the law?" Make note, Jesus does not rebuke him for asking this question.

In a parallel passage, Mark 12: 32-34 the scribe repeats Jesus' answer with commentary and Christ gives him a praise. "And the scribe said unto him, Well, Master, thou hast said the truth: for there is one God; and there is none other but he: And to love him with all the heart, and with all the understanding, and with all the soul, and with all the strength, and to love his neighbour as himself, is more than all whole burnt offerings and sacrifices. And when Jesus saw that he answered discreetly, he said unto him, Thou art not far from the kingdom of God," (Mark 12:32-34). This is high praise indeed from Christ to those who were opposed to his Kingdom.[2] There is a certain amount of knowledge that will bring a man up to the door of the King's castle, but he is still one inch from being inside. Even if he is a mile from the door, it is of little consequence in the end

---

[2] See my work, *The Kingdom of Heaven is Upon You*, for a full discussion of Christ's understanding of the Kingdom of Heaven, or Kingdom of God.

if it leads one to hell; an inch or a mile still deposits him into the same place.

The question asked concerned the debate over the *greatest* commandment. Would asking such a question be of utmost importance? It would have been in Jesus' day that the rabbis would debate such things; which commandment, which of the 613 commandments, 248 positive, 365 negative, was "the great," the *greatest* and best commandment that God has ever given his people? Certainly, God would have had it transmitted and written down. This seems like a reasonable question. In this way, from the scribe's perspective, the moral law, ceremonial law and judicial law were combined in his question. The greatest commandment God has ever given lies somewhere in "these laws," he thought. Christ, knowing his mission to fulfill *all* righteousness, directed this law expert, this scribe, to consider the moral law, and in it, its two parts, with a commentary.

In verses 37–40, "He answered him, You shall love the Lord your God with all your heart and with all your soul and with all your mind. This is the great and first commandment. And a second like it is this: You shall love your neighbor as yourself. On these two commandments depend the whole law and the prophets." Christ directs the law expert to the God of the whole bible. The whole duty of man, the whole moral-spiritual law of God that shows forth his attributes and character, can be summed up in considering the disposition of the man to the will of God in Scripture, as it is equally attested to in the summation of the whole Scripture in the Moral law – everything rests on it. The one answer is an answer to all the written and spoken words. Such a disposition is found in the one who *loves God* and *loves his neighbor* which is a *summary* of the word. It is not merely about words on a page, but the disposition and action of the one who knows the word and then acts in accordance with it. The summary surrounds *love* (which is the greatest of all gifts of the Spirit) and this is then directed into the heart of the Moral Law. *Love* is the whole of the law summed up in a word. Not any kind of love will do, but the love that demonstrates the heart, soul and mind given over to love God without reservation, which in turn exercises itself as it lives in the world in a particular manner.[3] (That "particular manner" will be discussed later.)

Jesus, as he always did, took his answer from written Scripture, and the *Shema* of Deuteronomy, something that would have been repeated by the Jews daily. Notice that Jesus *does not do* certain things here. He does not tell this lawyer that it is a bad question. He does not say, "what do you mean sir ... we are in the process as a result of my coming to earth to write the New Testament now, and we have no time for this Old Testament Law." He does not say anything against the Old Testament. He does not say he disannuls that "old"

---

[3] See also Rom. 13:9-10; 1 Cor. 13.

law. He does not overthrow it. He does not do away with it as if he or his disciples ought *not* to uphold it. Instead, he confirms it, and he confirms it *radically*. To think highly of the law of God is to think highly of God and his word, it is, as Jesus explains, to love God in fact.

Jesus says that such eminent love is directed toward God and toward man. "And thou shalt love the Lord thy God with all thine heart, and with all thy soul, and with all thy might," (Deut. 6:5). This is what God had said through his prophet, Moses. Also, "Thou shalt not avenge, nor bear any grudge against the children of thy people, but thou shalt love thy neighbour as thyself: I am the Lord," (Lev. 19:18). He says that such a love is all encompassing and all captivating. Heart, soul, and mind must work in unison to love God, *and* to love one's neighbor; if they reject his law or are *law-less*,[4] they do not love God, and they do not love their neighbor. The heart is the seat of affections of the whole man. The soul is the spiritual side of the affections, with its emotions as they are enflamed to please God, both in its disposition and its attitude for exercising itself in love. The mind is the choice and will of a man. To will to do something is *the mind choosing*. In the Hebrew of Deut. 6:5 the reading is "heart, soul, and might," (meaning with great force). Mark 12:30 records "heart, soul, mind, and strength," summarizing the same thing. The overarching

---

[4] Isa. 3:5–8; Gal. 5:13, 14; 2 Pet. 2:10–19; Jude 1:8–13; Deut. 12:8; Judges 17:6, 21:25. "...depart from me, ye that work iniquity," (Matt. 7:23), *i.e.* lawlessness.

point in all these parallel passages is that Jesus says the whole man is devoted to this love of God and love of their neighbor.

When exclamation is intended, often in Scripture, words and phrases are repetitive. All the heart, all the soul, all the mind. The whole heart, the whole soul, the whole mind. Jesus rejects the notion in this repetition that God will be served in halves, or partially. Serving God in halves, serving God partially, is a sign of hypocrisy, and Jesus pronounced many woes against hypocrites.[5]

This great commandment which he gives is called the *greatest* because it rests in a twofold understanding of the Moral Law of God, which summarizes *all of the word of God.* It is the hinge on which the entire Scripture sits and swings. In fact, Jesus says the whole "law and the prophets" hang on this; hang on his words; as we will come to see, both the law and the answer to this scribe are *his* words. Everything God has ever written down hangs on this notion to the law's relationship to loving God. To remove love and the

---

[5] "But woe unto you, scribes and Pharisees, hypocrites! for ye shut up the kingdom of heaven against men: for ye neither go in yourselves, neither suffer ye them that are entering to go in," (Matt. 23:13). There are many instances of hypocrites in Scripture, or acting hypocritically, or pretending, such as when Jacob impersonated Esau and deceived his father, (Gen. 27). Joseph's deception of his brethren, (Gen. 42–44). The false prophets of Ezek. 13:1–23. Judas, (Matt. 26:25, 48). Ananias and Sapphira, (Acts 5:1–10). Simon Magus, (Acts 8:18–23). Judaizing Christians in Galatia, (Gal. 6:13). False teachers at Ephesus, (Rev. 2:2).

twofold perception of the greatest command of God is to miss the promises of God as good, faithful, loving, gracious, merciful though all the Scripture. If the Scriptures tell God's people anything, anything from Genesis to Malachi, from Christ's perspective at this point in time, all that which God requires comes from a full love to God, and all this is tied to why men do what they do, what men do, and how they do it. There is the vertical relationship which the person has with God where they love God, and the Moral Law demonstrates how this love is to be exercised to him. Then, there is the horizontal relationship that men have with others each day as part of the body of the church, and in this they demonstrate love to others. Both are housed in the Moral Law, both are housed in Scripture, and both are housed in Christ's answer. The entire Bible sits on this notion of love.

The twofold aspect to Christ's answer, is taken from a *summary of the law of God*. The Moral Law, comprised of ten words, or ten commandments, is set in two tables. Table one concerns the object, the means, the manner and time of worship to God (the first four commands). Loving God is explained thoroughly in the first table, in every way, from, every possible angle, annexed to those commands. Table two concerns actions in light of the first table, to love and act in accordance with morality to one's neighbors. Jesus does not recreate a *new* law, but explains, most sublimely, what the Moral Law *means*. Yet, "A new commandment

I give unto you, That ye love one another; as I have loved you, that ye also love one another," (John 13:34). Is this new? Or is it new by way of *perspective* because the Christ has now attached to it the fulfillment of the Law by his work and merit? This is why the Apostle John in explaining this new commandment says in 1 John 2:7 that it is *not new*, but that, from this new perspective, it is considered *fresh*. "Brethren, I write no new commandment unto you, but an old commandment which ye had from the beginning. The old commandment is the word which ye have heard from the beginning," (1 John 2:7).

The Moral Law is refreshed in this light by Christ, 1 John 2:8, "Again, a new commandment I write unto you, which thing is true in him and in you: because the darkness is past, and the true light now shineth," because it comes from the lips of God incarnate. *All* this, to love God and to love one's neighbor, is the whole of the Scripture's teaching, as it has *always* been. It is the whole reformation of the redeemed man to newness of life if it is kept as God requires in love to him. This is the greatest of those things which God commands of his people.[6]

---

[6] In order to understand this, even in part, this chapter, and three following, are really one long treatise, divided into four parts, or four chapters. It would take too long to get to the substance of this idea in one chapter, so the whole treatise is divided for sake of time in 4 parts. My original intent was simply to set down the idea presented in *chapter 3* on the *heart, soul and mind*. But in order to get to that place, we have to traverse the first two chapters for an inclusive context. And, we have to consider chapter 4, then, in light of the

Christ requires the complete reformation of the whole man in light of his law of love. Is Jesus out of his mind? Commandments? Why is Jesus answering the lawyer by way of *commandments*? Why didn't he just tell him there is *no law to follow now*, there is *only grace?* Why wasn't his answer, "You are mistaken sir, the law is over?" Are men to be obedient to God's commandments in Exodus 20? *The 1647 Westminster Confession of Faith* in 19:5 says, "The moral law doth forever bind all, as well justified persons as others, to the obedience thereof; and that not only in regard of the matter contained in it, but also in respect of the authority of God the Creator who gave it. Neither doth Christ in the gospel any way dissolve, but much strengthen, this obligation." This has confused a great many professing Christians in the church throughout history. And many confused people who have thrown away the law (lawlessness) have tried to give sensible answers, but have failed in doing so. Some say that Jesus meant that loving God and loving your neighbor was only in regards to Old Testament saints; which is nonsense, (but this is certainly an attempt at being theologically clever). Some say that Jesus only meant this for the time he walked the earth, and then when the Apostle Paul came along, things changed where the law

---

first 3 chapters, which then, makes more sense to follow the order and sequence of these ideas as I have laid them out. We would not understand what Christ meant, or some of the important nuances which we will cover here by jumping to "heart, soul and mind."

was thrown out, which is equally nonsense. (And not very clever at all.) Some say Jesus was merely gratifying the Pharisees, which meant he lied, which is utterly nonsense, and abominable.

So, right out of the gate, an objection must first be dispelled if Jesus' words are to be understood. It can be summed up in the words of the Apostle Paul in Rom. 6:14, which is the Antinomian's contextual banner, "For ye are not under the Law." Now, Antinomians neglect to quote the beginning of the verse, and only refer to the end. "For sin shall not have dominion over you: for ye are not under the law, but under grace," (Rom. 6:14). But Jesus just referred his hearers *to the law*, to love God and love their neighbor *by the law,* in the light of the law, through the law, which is, in fact, the greatest command he could ever give. One must ask the Antinomian, was Jesus confused? Paul in Romans 6 is certainly referring to the Moral Law, which contains in it the whole duty of man to God. But what does it mean to be "under the law?" Paul never says that one is *released* from obedience to the law, but released from *the reign of the power of the law and sin* over sinners when they are converted. Any sin, that reigns to death, the Christian is released from its condemning power. Paul never says it is okay now to worship other gods, or use the Lord's name in vain, or to profane the Sabbath, or to lie, or to kill, or to covet, *etc.* What *Christian* would ever say that? Where does Paul ever say that? They are no longer, as Adam did in the Garden, *to work for justification before God;*

Adam has already blown it in that capacity, and fallen men can never do it.

The Moral Law condemns all sinners in their sinful state and in their sins if they still try to justify themselves by works to be saved.[7] It is impossible because they are fallen; legalism is condemned; but obedience to Christ the King is *never* condemned. Who are these people that Paul speaks about that are not under the Law? Believers, justified and separated people, born again Christians who are made alive to God by the Spirit of Jesus Christ. These believers are dead to sin now, and they do not allow sin to reign in them, for they are unshackled by Christ's power. They have been made alive to God in Jesus Christ by grace and are no longer under the *condemning power* of the Law. Believers, through Christ, have been delivered from the condemning power of God's holy character which exposes their sinfulness and shows their wickedness and fallen nature. They cannot *work* their way into heaven and then stand before God demanding he owes them a debt. Before they were converted, they, like the scribe Jesus spoke to, were committing outward actions in hopes of pleasing God. God will never accept this because of the fall. But the privilege of all born again believers, Old Testament or New Testament, is that Christ has fulfilled everything they had to do to be justified before God. Christ was made under the Law, to redeem those that were under the Law, that they might

---

[7] We call this, legalism – to work for salvation to get into heaven.

receive the adoption of sons, (Gal. 4:4). Why? ... for their sanctification? No, *for their justification.* They are redeemed by him and are no longer under the Law to work to be accepted before God. If anyone is still under the Law, all those still under Adam, they are under the curse. All born-again believers, are not under the curse, because what Christ did was save them through his death and resurrection, his regenerating Spirit, and gave them the justifying faith of Abraham by grace.[8] They are not under the Law to save themselves, they are not under its condemning nature, because Christ has saved them; he is the Savior, he is the Deliverer.

Christians cannot be like the scribes who work for salvation in light of the Law (hypocrites and legalists). All born again believers have the Spirit of Christ dwelling in them after conversion.[9] And Paul will later say, "For as many as are led by the Spirit of God, they are the sons of God," (Rom. 8:14). They are not under the Law for justification; they can work no work to earn their way into heaven, to get into the pearly gates. There is nothing they can do to earn an entrance or ticket into celestial glory. These believers have eternal life by promise, and (because of Christ) by inheritance.[10] They have not worked for eternal life, or pleased God to

---

[8] See Romans 4-5.
[9] "...but ye know him; for he dwelleth with you, and shall be in you," (John 14:17).
[10] "And if children, then heirs; heirs of God, and joint-heirs with Christ," (Rom. 8:17). And "...heirs according to the promise," (Gal. 3:29).

such an extent that God now owes them something because of some justifying work they did. They are freed by Christ from being under the condemnation of the Law. "For if the inheritance be of the law, it is no more of promise: but God gave it to Abraham by promise," (Gal. 3:18). Yet then the question arises, what purpose then does the Law serve the Christian? Why did Jesus go to the Law to answer the scribe's question?

There a couple of points to consider first before answering those questions in full. If one is under the Law they are under the curse of God. The Law condemns the natural man at every turn. He tries to lift himself up to some happiness in this life, but all he does is wrap the straight jacket of the curse around himself tighter, his efforts turn into a further curse; he aggravates it. He has no comfort, will receive no comfort, unless he is born again from above (John 3), for comfort only comes from the Spirit *after* being born again. It only comes from justification, which will in turn lead him to happiness because he will then press into the kingdom in *holiness*. To the natural man the Law is a bolt of lightning, which strikes over and over and over in the same place while they live under it. There are only so many things in the world to try and ease the pain of the fall; money, fame, health, family, work. In fact, the carnal man tries his best to sear his conscience with all these things so that the Law of God will not spoil the supposed pleasures of sin for him while he lives on earth.[11] If one is under the Law,

---

[11] "...having their conscience seared with a hot iron," (1 Tim. 4:2).

it stops entrance into heaven, and all the blessings of God. It is a very solemn Scripture in the prophet Isaiah, where he says, "Therefore hell hath enlarged herself, and opened her mouth without measure: and their glory, and their multitude, and their pomp, and he that rejoiceth, shall descend into it," (Isa. 5:14). Hell's mouth is opened wide for the natural man. It does not matter what he amasses in this life, hell will take it in, and the Apostle James in expounding this says that all those things will be a witness against them into eternity. "Your gold and silver is cankered; and the rust of them shall be a witness against you, and shall eat your flesh as it were fire. Ye have heaped treasure together for the last days," (James 5:3). Glory, quantity of possessions, fame, pomp; they are useless to gain acceptance before God. If one is under the Law, they are under the thumb of their father the devil. Of the scribes and Pharisees Christ said, "Ye are of your father the devil, and the lusts of your father ye will do," (John 8:44). They serve and work by his power and will. Natural men are forced to serve the devil and his lusts, being of the same family, and children of wrath, as Jesus said. If one is under the curse of the Law, this life is only the beginning of sorrows. It is all curse, death, sting and pain. From death, hell follows thereafter, which is the sting of death for the wicked.[12] Miseries begin in this life, and enhance into the afterlife. If a man dies under the

---

[12] "...and his name that sat on him was death, and hell followed with him," (Rev. 6:8).

condemnation of the Law, there is nothing blessed to expect; only death without mercy.

So, then the question is asked, "How does a person get out from under the Law?" There is no reformation of life without getting out from under the condemnation of the Law. It would be a fruitless endeavor to speak about loving God with all the heart, soul and mind, if one is still under the Law and working for their justification and acceptance before God. They must get out from under it before they can ever experience reformation in their life. Men are delivered from being under the curse of the Law by two graces which are worked by the Spirit of God in their soul because of what Christ did. Consider both faith and repentance which lead to obedience.

The born-again Christian's life may certainly be summed up as *love God and love your neighbor;* all those who are like faithful Abraham are like this. Only that kind of person, a born-again person, a born-again Abraham, a born-again Jacob, a born-again Samson, a born-again David, a born-again Solomon, is able to do such things as King Jesus commands. But in order to take time to understand *obedience* in that way, loving God and loving your neighbor, people must first come to faith; if they are not in the faith, they cannot love God, or their neighbor, or press into Christ's kingdom in any godly way.

Faith in the Christ is first. "Then he said, "Lord, I believe!" And he worshiped him," (John 9:38), and here saving faith as a confession is *a sure knowledge and hearty trust of all that God has revealed in his Word, which the Holy Spirit works in men by the Gospel, where forgiveness of sins, everlasting righteousness, and salvation are freely given by God, merely of grace, only for the sake of Christ's work and merits.* What is the born again Christian to have faith in? Part of that answer is Christ's work in righteousness in fulfilling the Law for them. Faith is that which establishes the Law because it believes that only in Jesus Christ there is forgiveness and remission of sin; they are saved by Christ's works who fulfilled the Law perfectly for them. It believes in the heart, soul and mind that Jesus Christ reckons to the sinner's account his righteous work, his work as a garment, and that all the sin of the sinner is reckoned to Christ, and that his righteousness is exchanged for their sin. They believe he has given them a garment of salvation that wraps them up, and he graciously takes away their sin. God punishes the Christ for their sin instead of them. Such a faith is the sinner now believing, as Abraham was believing as the father of the faithful. Such a faith, is a firm and constant apprehension of Christ and all his merits, as they are promised and offered in his word and in his sacraments, in his good tidings of the Gospel.[13] It is a faith that can never be lost; it is how they live as new creatures. Rom. 1:17 says, "The just shall live by faith." It is a justifying faith, because it

---

[13] See my work, *The Five Principles of the Gospel,* for a full discussion of what constitutes the "good news."

enables the elect soul to receive Christ's perfect justice to salvation for their whole life. It is the justifying power that allows them entrance into the King's Kingdom both here and now, and ultimately into heaven. This faith once obtained, is never utterly lost. It can waiver at times, but it is *never lost.* It can be made more or less by degree, but it is *never lost.* It is described and defined in this way by Scripture, repeatedly, Rom. 5:1, "faith whereby we are justified." Eph. 2:8, faith through which we are saved. 1 Tim. 1:5, faith unfeigned. Gal. 5:6, faith which works by love. Acts 15:9, faith that purifies the heart. And what kind of faith is this that justifies? 2 Peter 1:1, *faith which is precious.* After conversion, this faith turns a corner, and it then increases by degrees, Rom. 1:17, being in some strong and great, Luke 7:9, in others weak and small, Matt. 14:31. But it can now *never* be lost *if it is true faith.* And it turns the heart, soul and mind, to a life of penitent service before the throne of King Jesus; this is initially called repentance, the next step in conversion.

Repentance is turning to God through Christ by the power of the Spirit, by faith, to follow the King's commands. Man, under the curse, is in grave danger. The fall of Adam has placed him in the worst possible position, for "in Adam all die." Man must escape this curse or bear its full penalty from an infinite God who has been abused time and time again by such sordid lives of those who rebel against him and his Law; man must repent of this. As the 1647 Westminster Larger

26

Catechism says, in Question 76: "What is repentance unto life? Answer: Repentance unto life is a saving grace, wrought in the heart of a sinner by the Spirit and word of God, whereby, out of the sight and sense, not only of the danger, but also of the filthiness and odiousness of his sins, and upon the apprehension of God's mercy in Christ to such as are penitent, he so grieves for and hates his sins, as that he turns from them all to God, purposing and endeavoring constantly to walk with him in all the ways of new obedience." Is this not a simple idea, that in reality, is exactly what Christ is explaining? A life of loving God is a faithful life which is *penitent* before him. Repentance *is a change of the mind*, strictly defined. It is to think very differently about life and godliness once faith takes hold of the heart, soul and mind. It is linked to godly sorrow; sometimes Scripture uses that phrase for the whole of repentance, as with Manasseh when he was filled with sorrow and so became a new man, (2 Chron. 33:12).[14] It is a breaking of the heart under the realization of the Spirit's direction that one has displeased God and broken his Law. It is true, it is to become wise, after the fact. The one repenting desires, with godly grief, something which *has* been done, to be *undone*, because they see the great hurt that comes from it against God. It is to change the mind being saddened and shamed for sin (as it is sin and an offence of God, and infinitely so). In it, there is purpose, purpose of

---

[14] "For godly sorrow worketh repentance to salvation not to be repented of," (2 Cor. 7:10).

reformation and amending of one's life; sight, sorrow, confession, shame, hatred and turning from sin. All these make up repenting.

"Thus saith the Lord GOD; Repent, and turn yourselves from your idols; and turn away your faces from all your abominations," (Ezek. 14:6). Did he just say "all your abominations;" did Jesus say with all your heart, soul and mind? In this the soul is greatly humbled. Holy Job said, "Wherefore I abhor myself, and repent in dust and ashes," (Job 42:6). It is to know the plague of a man's own heart discerned by the power of Christ's Spirit in him by faith. "...which shall know every man the plague of his own heart," (1 Kings 8:38). It is to sow in tears, (Psa. 126:5), to confess and forsake sin, (Prov. 28:13), *all* of it. In it the duty required is *to change*, to make the change now, to do it because Christ says that one is to love God in the heart, soul and mind in penitent faith. "Now God commandeth all men every where to repent," to change now. It causes a person to run away, in haste, from the eternal damning sentence of the Law, and knocks at the wicket gate of Christ's mercy. The soul looks for pardon and forgiveness in this, looking to be pulled onto the road of salvation quickly, where all his sins will finally be removed by the mere gaze of the cross, and all his sins will be cancelled, taken by the Christ, falling off their back as a burden, and rolling into the grave of the open tomb; but after the tomb, there is more of a road.

The highway of salvation is a long road. But initial repentance repeals all the condemnation of the Law for justification before God, and it casts all their sins into the sea of forgetfulness, never to be remembered by God any more, (Micah 7:19). They know at the judgment, the red, bleeding hand of the only Savior will have covered all their sins, and their repentance and life shows that blessed grace and change – everyone that enters heaven is saved by Christ for justification in the exact same way and to the exact same degree. All born again believers get into heaven by his work and merit exactly the same way, to the exact same degree. So, consider ... there must be a complete reformation of the whole man in light of Christ's Law of love.

Such a complete reformation renders a man a new creature. When faith and repentance take hold by the power of God's Spirit, men are made new; this is how *radical* the change is in them. The soul knows that they are justified by faith, not by the works of the Law. But the soul also knows the Law will then play some important part in their life, *i.e.* the will of God, the words of God, sanctify them after they are freed by Christ; they don't act like they did before, they are now new; how new? Radically new. The soul knows this because they were one way, heathenish, sons of the devil, and now they are no longer that way, they are new, they are changed. They no longer want to swear, or fornicate, or steal, now they want to honor God. They know this, even if they don't know how to orderly set this down in their mind. All believers are justified, and then they are all placed on the highway of *holiness.* Otherwise, if reformation were not required, if holiness were not required after one is converted, to cease to do evil and learn to do good, and that changed life were not true, everyone, all at the same time, would be made perfectly holy, instantaneously and all to the same degree in sanctification; but this is not what God does. He does not sanctify everyone all at the same time and to the same degree at their conversion. Sanctification is not justification. And to make them more holy Christ has given a single commandment to follow that will work holiness in this, for he has given them his Law. There are three uses to this Law: Use 1, to earn righteousness (either by Adam's failed attempt or by Christ's faithful work). Use 2, to guide fallen society in righteousness. Use 3, to sanctify justified people. If the Law no longer mattered, Jesus is a liar, his answer was wrong, and it was sinful. If the Law no longer mattered there would be no degrees of faithfulness, and no degrees of reward once people get to heaven; rewarded by holy works. Sanctification would be a myth and believers would all be perfect at the very same time, the moment they are saved to the very same degree. In fact, all the Scriptural talk about rewards and heaven in that way would be lost by this *Antinomian* idea. Remember, Antinomians are against the Law. They say, "Don't tell me to be up and doing to assure me of my election by works, for all I need is Jesus," they think.

By brief way of reminder, Antinomians speak this way and have all through the history of the Christian church. "Well, if sanctification is all about us sinning less and less, then we would have to conclude that the Holy Spirit isn't doing his job very well." This is blasphemous talk. "God can never be disappointed in you or surprised by your sin if he is the one controlling the entire process of growth from start to finish." "Contrary to popular belief, our spiritual growth is not up to us, nor is the spiritual growth of the people around us." "God is not captivated by our attempts to please him." "Obeying God is far beyond our ability even after becoming a Christian." Those statements are a willful violation of the third commandment, and take God's holy name in vain. They are diametrically opposed to all of Christ's teaching, and they are opposed to the Gospel. This is not the way the Christ speaks; it is not the way the Bible speaks, it is not the way Christians speak. Christ tells men to love God and love their neighbor, and directs them straight into the hands of proving out one's faith by their holiness as they stand in relation to his Law. Justified people who are no longer under the Law press into the kingdom,[15] otherwise there would be no need of *pressing*. Paul speaks the very same way, "Do we then make void the Law through faith? God forbid: yea,

---

[15] "I press toward the mark for the prize of the high calling of God in Christ Jesus," (Phil. 3:14).

we establish the Law," (Rom. 3:31); we cause it to stand before us *because we walk in it.* Pause there in our study for a moment. Let's consider this in our walk as it relates to a general consideration of the complete reformation of man in light of Christ's Law of love.

Radical transformation gives way to reformation ... that is step 1 for you in considering a holy life as a Christian. What is this maxim but "saved, and then reforming;" for reformation of life is just that, a reform of your life. And it is not done in an instant; sanctification is not instant like justification is. Otherwise you would be as sanctified as the next person, and that, instantaneously at conversion; and you very well know Scripture does not bear that out, and personally you know the truth of it. Your justification is not your sanctification.

In considering this, I'm not speaking about holiness as it relates to justification by faith alone. That's already done in you as a believer. I'm speaking about holiness, which is what Christ was speaking about, in your life. Now, don't throw the book down and yell, "Legalist!" This is not legalism. Legalism is trying to *earn salvation.* No, this is godly, holy obedience to King Jesus. Not just that he is Savior, but that he is your Lord and King.

Antinomianism is common and endemic today in Christian evangelicalism. People will say and think, "Don't tell me about works, doing, living, holiness; loosen up, Jesus has got this for you." Such people completely miss the third use of the Law for the Christian. Listen to what Calvin wrote on this,

> The third use of the Law is associated to you as a believer in whose hearts the Spirit of God already reigns. You are motioned by the Spirit where you desire to obey God, and two ways in which you still profit in the Law. It teaches you with greater truth and certainty what the will of the Lord is which you desire to follow and to confirm you in this knowledge. Then, you gain further knowledge by frequently meditating on it, and will be excited and moved to obedience, and confirmed in that obedience, and drawn away from all the slippery paths of sin. In this way you as a saint hasten toward righteousness. But those who are impaired by the sluggishness of the flesh make less progress than they ought. The Law acts like a whip to the flesh, urging it on. Some unskillful people boldly throw away the whole Law of Moses, and do away with both its Tables, imagining it unchristian to adhere to a doctrine which contains what they think of as the administration of death; this is because they miss the Law in its sanctifying use. Our thoughts should be far from this profane notion. It is ungodly to discard it. Less duty is not the aim of the Christian, Jesus pressed us to do more. Our whole life is a race, and after we have finished our

course, the Lord will enable us to reach the goal. The Law has the force of exhortation, not to bind your consciences with a curse, but by urging you, to shake off laziness and imperfection and to strive to be more holy; there are rewards for such work. When the Lord declares, that he did not come to destroy the Law, but to fulfil (Matt. 5:17); that until heaven and earth pass away, not one jot or tittle shall remain unfulfilled; he shows that his coming was not to dissuade you in any degree from the observance of the Law. The doctrine of the Law has not been infringed by Christ, but remains, that, by teaching, admonishing, rebuking, and correcting, it may fit and prepare us for every good work.[16]

The Law never binds us to justifying condemnation, but it is our sure guide of holiness before Christ; it causes you to consider, "am I that way, or not? Am I what Christ said I should be in light of salvation?"

In question 97 of the Larger Catechism, it asks, "What special use is there of the moral Law to the regenerate? Answer: ... to conform themselves thereunto as the rule of their obedience." In other words, obedience shows their thankfulness to Christ for fulfilling the Law, so now they are obedient to it.

---

[16] Calvin, John, *Institutes of the Christian Religion*, (Bellingham, WA: Logos Bible Software, 1997), 2:7:12.

People wonder why they don't grow in their spiritual walk with Christ, that they don't see growth and conclude, years into such a walk, that they think it is normal not to grow. "Last year I was the same as this year," they think. Two years ago, or five years ago, they are the same as they are now. They do the same things, and think the same way, and think that pressing into the kingdom is just holding on to the *status quo.* And yet, they then wonder why the church is not effective in its ministry in the world, in prayer, in growing as students of the word, *etc.*? It is because they misuse the idea of the Law, they do not go to it and do not understand what Christ did for them and their response to it in obedience. They do not consider it. God never says my people are destroyed by a lack of grace, but destroyed by a lack of knowing and doing (Hosea 4:6). Every time God chastises his people in the word, they don't know something, and they neglect to do something.

I want you to set these three uses of the Law as outlined in the Westminster Confession in your mind. [1] The 'first use' of the Law is to convict of sin and drive you as a repentant sinner to the Lord Jesus Christ; you cannot be justified by the Law before God because you are fallen (Adam blew this for all men, so men now need the Christ who will work for you for your justification); you are saved by works of the Law, by Christ's works of the Law for you - justified. But after that ... after you have the Christ ... there's more, and the more is a sign post to tell you whether you have the Christ or not, which is sanctification.

[2] The 'second use' of the Law is to restrain Lawlessness. Which is why people who murder, or extortioners, or rapists, or people who commit libel go to jail, or are fined, or such things. Laws are made in society to stop sin; to oversimplify it, this is what the divines called the general equity of the Law, which is stated in our confession. How do these biblical Laws apply to society? The Law is applied to society for the good of society; murderers should go to jail, society should be structured in a way to use that general equity.

[3] But the 'third use' of the Law is to function as the rule of life for you as a Christian, to show you whether you fulfill Christ's commands to love God or not. One of the most famous 17th century historical statements of this truth comes from the Puritan and Westminster Divine Samuel Bolton in his work, "The True Bounds of Christian Freedom," where he said, "The Law sends us to the gospel for our justification; then the gospel sends us to the Law to frame our whole way of life."[17] Your sanctification is bound in it. Without it, and the Holy Spirit working it in and for you, you will *not* be sanctified. Without it you will never grow because growing in Christ is not being magically zapped by the Holy Spirit while you sleep in your bed at night – it surrounds being embolden in the constituted means of

---

[17] Bolton, Samuel, *The Moral Law: A Rule of Obedience*, http://www.the-highway.com/articleFeb00.html.

grace he has given you and you are to be exercised in them; without which there is no sanctification. People wonder why they don't grow, that they are not gaining ground from one week to another, from one month to another, from one year to another, it is because they *misuse* the means of grace. They are content to be Antinomian in their life.

Antinomianism teaches that since salvation is entirely of grace and cannot be lost once it has been received, then why bother about keeping the commandments? Why make life harder? So, these never growing people continue a cycle - what is this cycle – it is this - sin, forgiveness; sin, forgiveness, sin and forgiveness, never growing, where their lives never are for the better, never change; or, worse, that cycle causes them to regress backwards and fall away in apostasy because they *don't grow*. This is the very point of Christ's words, as much as it is the Apostle's, as much as Paul said, in Romans 6, from those who admonished continuance in sin so that grace may abound. No. *Sin ... forgiveness*, over and over with *no* growth; that's *never* Jesus's answer. It is what carnal men want to believe about their life, because it is easier to ask forgiveness than permission; that is *not* a Christian concept.

Antinomianism wants nothing to do with holiness, but argues that the way to grow in grace, to promote sanctification and holiness of life is not by keeping the commandments – they think: One antinomian said, "Sanctification is the sovereign work of

the Holy Spirit; we must walk in the Spirit."
Antinomians believe they are zapped into holiness by
the sovereignty of the Spirit. When they say things like
that, they are saying, we must be zapped by the
sovereign Holy Spirit in some manner which is
unknown to us in order to wake up one morning more
holy than we did the day before because sanctification is
the Spirit's job not mine. No, Scripture does not teach
that; he who begun the work completes it in all born
again believers (Phil 1:6). Why? How? What tools will
he use? I don't find the word "zap" in Philippians there.
New Covenant Theology today, which is not really
covenant theology, blatantly teaches this heretical
position. We are 'New Testament Christians' they plea.
Any relationship with the Law is over; it doesn't matter
what Jesus said about it. They are against what Christ is
teaching in loving God and loving your neighbor ... who
is teaching them to keep the Law of God, of which all the
Law and prophets hang, which all justified Christians
press and strive and walk in.

How do you know you are out from under the
condemning nature of God's Law? Many people will
merely give an answer with no proof to this very serious
question. What will *you* do with that question? Are you
out from under the Law's condemnation? Antinomians
say, "I am not under the Law, but under grace." "I know
I am" they say, and so I ask them, "How do you know?"
"Well, I know because I know." I tell them at that point,
they have no idea what they are saying; Jesus doesn't

ever say that your answer to the faith that lies within you, that radical change to a new creature, is to know because you know. People like that are parroting a verse or two in the Scriptures, without really understanding what they mean by it, or what is meant by Scripture's statement. Paul answers against those people, "For I bear them record that they have a zeal of God, but not according to knowledge," (Rom. 10:2). They don't know what they are saying.

The biblical answer lies in certain marks (in Jesus' words, fruitfulness), which we can consider by asking just four questions. 1. Are you subject to the Gospel and its power? This is the same as asking, do you grow in the knowledge and obedience of the Gospel? "What do you mean by that," you might ask? I mean do you grow in knowledge and obedience because of God's gracious work in you. Are you more knowledgeable this year than last, and are you more obedient this year than last, is the Spirit working and are you concurring in your sanctification? How can you tell, and what shows you that it's so? Love God and love your neighbor, as we will consider further later on, is not inactive – it is an action word that requires resolve. If a person does not obey the Gospel of Christ, can he be saved? Jesus says ... in no way.

Jesus never says be assured of your salvation by considering the "theory of election." He says look at your works because good trees that have been saved by him, will produce good fruit. Sell all you have and follow me. Multiply more talents while I'm gone. Put your hand to the plow and don't look back. Press into the kingdom. Strive to enter the narrow gate. Be watchful, take heed, be fruitful. Jesus was explaining the Law of loving God (love is an action word) to a lawyer. If one has a heart that is born again, they will then love God and love their neighbor as Jesus says, it is to be done according to his Law. They will take what Christ says in the Law, and like a mirror look in it and say, yes, that's me; I do that, and conclude, the Spirit is working in me in those things. The Apostle Paul concludes that such a person is still under the whole power of the Law, that really does not know and does not obey the Gospel of Christ, the Law of Christ. But *obey*, this is such a strange word attached to "saved by grace," isn't it, if misunderstood, if one mixes justification with sanctification. Which is why the 1647 Westminster Confession of Faith has whole sections, not mixed sections, on saving faith, repentance, good works, the Law of God, *etc.* Paul says that we are to "fulfil the Law of Christ," (Gal. 6:2). The Law of Christ is the Law of God; it's his Law. Jesus' words are very clear in loving God and loving your neighbor; that's *his* Law, his two tables in Exodus 20.

2. Are you walking worthy of the Gospel? The Antinomian shouts out, "Well no one does." Where does Jesus say that? Walking worthy is an important topic.[18] The bible is filled with a *theology of walking* before God. "Jesus answered, Are there not twelve hours in the day?

---

[18] See my books in the *5 Marks* series that cover various aspects of walking with God and Christ.

If any man walk in the day, he stumbleth not, because he seeth the light of this world. But if a man walk in the night, he stumbleth, because there is no light in him," (John 11:9-10). When teachings get hard people walk away, "From that time many of his disciples went back, and walked no more with him," (John 6:66). "He that ... hath withdrawn his hand from iniquity, hath executed true judgment between man and man, hath walked in my statutes, and hath kept my judgments, to deal truly; he is just, he shall surely live, saith the Lord GOD," (Ezek. 18:8-9). See, the end of all our freedom in Christ is a freedom from sin, a freedom *to be holy,* where you will then give God holy praise in keeping his Law to love him and love your neighbor; because *praise* is also an action word and is not merely done with the mouth, but with the life; a life of praise. In *Pilgrim's Progress,* you may remember Faithful being pummeled by an old man, and when Faithful inquired who the old man was, he cried out for mercy, and the old man, as he beat him senseless, said, "I am Moses and I know not how to show mercy." Bunyan was explaining the Law of God without Christ, without the Spirit, that righteous Law is merciless on an unconverted sinner because all it does is point out his sin, and beats him to death; he can't stand in God's holy presence without the garment of salvation. But to those who have it, the Law is pleasant and not burdensome with Jesus and his Holy Spirit; Christ even attests that his Law "is easy and light" for saved born-again people. Delivered and rejoicing in the Christ who frees you from the Law's condemnation, to be able, then, by the Spirit who lives in you to walk worthy of the Christ who saved you. Does not King Jesus deserve your obedience to him in this way to rejoice in your life, in your walk? Love to Christ necessary to escape the curse at his coming shows itself in love to God and love to one's neighbor. A person that never sets forth the act of loving God can't say he has the principle of Christ living in him. The Antinomian can say nothing; all his thoughts are all *theory*. God's Law without the Christ, without the shield and bucker of the Christ, is a cruel master truly, and only accuses you, curses you, terrifies you and condemns you; it will kill you. Initial faith, your first act repentance, caused you to change into a new man, not like the old one, now, very much to prize the garment of salvation that the Lord Jesus covers you with, setting you free from bondage, and presses you to press into the kingdom. And the heart, soul and mind are set free in Christ, gloriously cheerful in the exultant liberty that Christ has bestowed on them, not to sin, but to be, as Bolton said, led back to the Law of Christ to keep it; it frames your whole life to love God and others.

3. Do you have peace in your conscience? Some of you reading this might have never even thought about it. There is now peace of conscience for born again believers, those who have the Spirit of God dwelling in them. You might ask, "peace through the Law?" Of course! Where do you think assurance of election comes from? Your conscience was suppressed before because it

hated the Law and it was a *terror* to you; God was a terror through the Law. That old conscience you had, you pushed it down so that it didn't stir you up at all; it was like a dead man to you. You felt nothing in your conscience before when you sinned. You complained of nothing; you did not complain of a deficiency in holiness. There, as a deceived and yet falsely secure sinner you sat under the intolerable burden of uncountable sins; and you didn't care one bit. Your conscience was very quiet about it all, and the further you sinned, the more your conscience was seared, scarred, and unfeeling. But conscience now ... as you are born again, it is ruled by the Spirit of Christ who is a violent wind in your soul stirring up his words in your heart, soul and mind. Now your conscience is far from quiet. It discerns all kinds of spiritual things. It is alive and flowing with rivers of living water. It knows whether peace is being cultivated in Christ, or not, every day, and it yearns to follow Jesus more. It's always affected by what you do or not do, and how well you employ what you do; and you know it; grieving the Spirit, vexing the Spirit, rejoicing in Christ, resting in Christ. If you don't follow Christ in some duty, your conscience bites you; when the Spirit ministers to you in some holy duty you find it so very sweet. The Spirit of grace is always pouring over you and creating in you the blessedness of a spirit of mourning over remaining sin, which sin you hate. And from that sowing in tears arises the harvest of the Spirit's joy to further your reformation before the great King. You find all his work in you to better you, rewarding, pleasing, agreeable, pleasurable. "This is my beloved, and this is my friend" (Song 5:16). My beloved is my friend and my King. My Lord and my God, as Thomas confessed. I ask you only, examine yourself to consider, is that you? Is that a description of you as one justified by profession with the peace of the Spirit of Christ directing you in pleasing the Lord by love? In contrast, the Antinomian says, "I am a lover of God, I have the love of God in me, though I can't tell that ever I put forth one act of love towards him in all my life."[19]

4. Are you led by the Spirit? Anyone that is out from under the condemnation of the Law, gives himself up to the leading of the Spirit; and where will the Spirit lead you? He takes you *back* to the words of the Son of God, to frame your whole life. It is your very prayer, is it not, – hallowed be thy name – not in some generality, but by a petition in your daily prayers to be holy, it's the first petition, so that you can hallow the Father's name, because Christ knows that holiness leads to happiness for you. And to be led by the Spirit has certain ordinary qualities in it. The first is at conversion, who works faith and repentance in us. The second is in sanctification, to make you more holy. Does he not *press* you into the Kingdom, and do you not concur in that? The Spirit guides your heart, soul and mind, through spiritual

---

[19] Howe, John, *A Sermon Directing What We Are to Do, after Strict Enquiry Whether or No We Truly Love God,* (London: Printed for Thomas Parkhurst, 1696), 5.

persuasion that Christ's truths concerning the Law and the prophets, the word that you read, are true, to be followed, to be obeyed; it is "the Law of Christ" as a sweetness to your soul because you know that exercise in that will make you more like Jesus. And what born again Christian doesn't want to be more like the Savior, conformed to his image?

Don't despair in this, for God is in Christ to reconcile you to win hearts, to captivate souls to expand minds, to the love of God. The Spirit helps you to order your heart, soul and mind, with cheerfulness and rejoicing. How does he do that? What does he teach you? He is very powerful to help you with strong and mighty motions to take hold of Christ's intervening grace towards reformation; day by day by day. This leading of the Spirit is a daily course that God prescribes, "the will of God is your sanctification", that's God's will the apostles says, that Christ communicates power to the pardoned soul, and that the Spirit facilitates that power by persuading you that the Scriptures you read are true and you desire to concur in that sanctifying influence to be bettered; he even rewards you for such holy service. This strangely sounds as though Christ is directing you in his word to love him and live in a certain way, hating the world, and loving his Christ, by his Spirit to act and live and walk in holiness, to be imitators of God as dear children, to redeem the time because the days are evil, to make the most of your sojourning here in this world for the glory of the Christ because you love him. Christ commands the complete reformation of the whole man in light of his Law of love ... how? Jesus has lovingly told you how. "You shall love the Lord your God with all your heart and with all your soul and with all your mind. This is the great and first commandment. And a second like it is this: You shall love your neighbor as yourself. On these two commandments depend the whole Law and the prophets." But, 1) how is this to be done, and, 2) what does this Law of Christ particularly teach? This chapter will be, then, somewhat of a cliffhanger, and we will continue to answer this in the next chapter.

Chapter 2:
Reformation and Obedience

"Jesus said unto him, Thou shalt love the Lord thy God with all thy heart, and with all thy soul, and with all thy mind. This is the first and great commandment. And the second is like unto it, Thou shalt love thy neighbour as thyself," (Matt. 22:37-39).

Which is the great commandment in the Law? The twofold aspect to Christ's answer, is taken from a summary judgment of the Law of God and its application to *all* of the word of God. The Moral Law, comprised of ten commandments, is set in two tables; love God and love your neighbor. Table one concerns the object, the means, the manner and time of worship to God; that is loving God. Table two concerns actions in light of the first table, to love one's neighbor and act in accordance with morality to neighbors. Don't kill, honors parents, honor inferiors and superiors, do not envy or covet, no lying, *etc.* Jesus does not recreate a *new* Law, but explains what the Law means; he is often doing this in his teachings. And all this, to love God and to love one's neighbor, is the *whole* of the Scripture's teaching; all the Law and prophets *hang* on this truth.

So as much as the Bible teaches, whatever it teaches, the Bible is summarized into love God and love your neighbor, in this way, the bible is summarized in the ten commandments that Christ gave his church from the mount. To follow his commandments is the whole reformation of the man to newness of life if it is kept as God requires in love.[1] This is the greatest of those things which God commands of his people; to love him and to love others.

Be reminded then, Christ requires the complete reformation of the whole man in light of his Law of love. The Law of God commands and demands complete perfection, as it was from the beginning of creation. God is perfect, and requires his people to be perfect, this is the reflective use of the word "all". "All your heart," *etc.* This is the *entire* conformity of the moral nature and conduct of a rational creature with the nature and will of Jesus Christ. "Thou shalt love the Lord thy God with *all* thy heart, and with all thy soul, and with all thy mind," (Matthew 22:37). No one can in a fallen state accomplish this without the Spirit of Christ. Do not be confused, Jesus is telling people that they *can* love God, and ought to do so.

To clear this point, I have to remind you, for a moment, about the nature of the Moral Law of God which is, 1) universal,[2] 2) eternally binding, and 3) of a

---

[1] ὁ δὲ Ἰησοῦς ἔφη αὐτῷ, Ἀγαπήσεις κύριον τὸν θεόν σου, (Matt. 22:37).

[2] "The moral law, ... is of universal and perpetual obligation." Henry, Matthew, *Matthew Henry's Commentary on the Whole Bible: Complete and Unabridged in One Volume,* (Peabody: Hendrickson, 1994), xvi. And, "that universal justice which is described in the Moral Law remains." Calvin, John, *Institutes of the Christian Religion,* (Bellingham, WA: Logos Bible Software, 1997).

perpetual nature, as Scripture teaches[3] and *the 1647 Westminster Confession of Faith* reinforces.[4] "God intended by these ten words ... to oblige all Christians, to the world's end, to perpetual obedience, is clear."[5] The Law is universal, in that it is applied to all men for all time. Men must be like God, and be perfect, which is what the Lord points to (Matt. 5:48). It is forever binding because God is eternal.[6] All men must bow to King Jesus in this as the Great King who dispenses Law.

This Moral Law is perpetual because God is unchanging.[7] His word and will match his character forever. Christians pray that what occurs on earth is done, as it is done in heaven perfectly by men and angels in hallowing God's name. The Moral Law which is God's

---

[3] Matthew 22:40; Mark 12:29-33; Luke 10:27.

[4] *The Sum of Saving Knowledge* states, "That the believer be soundly convinced, in his judgment, of his obligation to keep the whole Moral Law, all the days of his life." *The 1647 Westminster Confession of Faith*, The Evidences of True Faith. And question 97 in the *Larger Catechism* says, "Question 97: What special use is there of the moral law to the regenerate? Answer: Although they that are regenerate, and believe in Christ, be delivered from the moral law as a covenant of works, so as thereby they are neither justified[b] nor condemned; yet, besides the general uses thereof common to them with all men, it is of special use, to show them how much they are bound to Christ for his fulfilling it, and enduring the curse thereof in their stead, and for their good; and thereby to provoke them to more thankfulness, and to express the same in their greater care to conform themselves thereunto as the rule of their obedience."

[5] Rutherford, Samuel, *A Survey of the Spiritual Antichrist Opening the Secrets of Familism and Antinomianism,* (London: J.D. & R.I., 1648), 5.

[6] Exod. 3:14; Psa. 111:3; Isa. 57:15; 1 Tim. 1:17; Heb. 13:8; Rev. 1:8, 4:8.

[7] Num. 23:19; 1 Sam. 15:29; Isa. 46:10; Mal. 3:6; Rom. 11:29; 2 Tim. 2:13; Heb. 6:18.

word commands perfect obedience to man in his nature and actions, and forbids anything contrary to it. Rom. 7:14, "We know that the Law is spiritual." The Law is not bad; the Law is *good* because it shows *what* God is. And men are required to mimic God in character and conduct, in knowledge, righteousness and holiness exercising dominion in the world.

This Moral Law has two parts, 1) love God, and, 2) love your neighbor when it is given to Moses on tablets of stone, where God commands obedience for reformation, and the condition which is binding all those to obedience. And all those people who seek eternal life by fulfilling the Law perfectly must do so in its *highest* degree and without fail at *any* point; but to covenant breakers, who break it at any point or in any degree earn everlasting death. Keep it or don't keep it. It is not merely *profess it*, but *do it*, which is an extremely important facet of what Christ is saying; and it is to be done to its *superlative level.* The tablets stand as a testimony crying out, "Which will you be?" "What will you earn?" "What do you do?" The Moral Law is, as William Perkins said, "an abridgement of the whole Law, and an abridgment of the Covenant of Works."[8] If you want to sum up the Covenant of Works for justification that Adam had in the garden it is, "do this and live." In the context of the garden, Adam was to keep

---

[8] Perkins, William, ed. Joel R. Beeke, Greg A. Salazar, and Derek W. H. Thomas, *The Works of William Perkins,* Volume 6, (Grand Rapids, MI: Reformation Heritage Books, 2018), 66.

covenant with God perfectly, and on the pain of death, by committing a single sin, he would be expelled from life, and death would result, both spiritual and physical. For Adam in the garden, in order to remain in God's favor, Adam had to work for his salvation, to be justified, and fulfill God's desires for him perfectly, and that desire is set in Law, for the Law is a demonstration of God's character; and Adam was to obey without fail. To keep the Law without fail is to *be* like God. God keeps his Law without fail; he's perfect. Adam was required to be just like God. But Adam did not do that, and instead, chose to shortcut holiness, and tried to be like God in a different way other than what God had commanded. He desired to finish the race in a way not prescribed by God.

It was the devil's plea in the garden, *you will be like God knowing good and evil; you don't need to do it God's way, God knows shortcuts are good.* And as a result of the fall, the Covenant of Works became a curse on all men, for all men are fallen in Adam and are perpetually, universally and unchangeably required, under this covenant, to keep the Law perfectly. But because they are fallen, they are condemned by it already the moment they are conceived in sin, being under the Law, "Behold, I was shapen in iniquity; and in sin did my mother conceive me," (Psa. 51:5). They are at conception under the condemnation of the Law. They must get out from underneath it. It curses them, and because they violate it every moment of every day, in every thought in every way, they are liable to all its curses and they cannot uphold it in their sinful and fallen nature; they even come forth from the womb speaking lies, (Psalm 58:3); which is hyperbole to the act but not the point; they are wicked and fallen from conception. But when God gave his abridgment of the Law, this Moral Law in Ten Commandments, to Moses, he gave it under the Covenant of Grace *after* the fall. It was a very gracious act for God to publish the Law in such a way as to be further explained, but not to republish the Law that men must work for salvation in and of themselves, or even to republish a Covenant of Works again. Many people think that about the Law of God, that it is merely a republication of what Adam had. That is blatantly not what God did in Scripture; nor is it what the Confession teaches. It is a very gracious thing, for God to explain and demonstrate what fallen sinners must do in order to be justified before God; even if they cannot do it. Yet, did Moses think that he could be justified by works? "And the Lord said unto Moses, ... thou hast found grace in my sight, and I know thee by name," (Exod. 33:17). Certainly, at no time did Moses think that he could work for his salvation and earn it and be justified before God. They need to be "justified by the Law" which is what the Law screams at them, "be justified before God" and it is true, God's character shows them what they must *be* in order to be perfect as their Father in heaven is perfect. But alas, they are unable to keep it; and they knew that. They always sin before God's face. What will they do? What do they look to but what God instructed them to look to, "The Lord make his face shine upon thee, and be gracious unto thee," (Num. 6:25). Grace in the Law? No, no, *the grace of the Law.* Moses says, "And these words which I command you today shall be in your heart," (Deut. 6:6), for the Law is *very* gracious to be given. But, if one is to stand on their own before God on the day of judgment according to the moral Law of God, to be justified they must stand in it perfectly. What true Israelite would think they have the power to accomplish that on their own? I will tell you, none of them did. Only hypocrites and false professors think they can do something to please God to gain justification, and this is because they are slaves to sin, and misuse the moral Law of God as a carnal commandment.

Christ alone fulfills the Moral Law of God for penitent believing sinners so they may love God and love one another. The blood of Christ alone is the only remedy able to cleanse filthy sinners from their original corruption. Salvation is only through the blood of Jesus Christ.[9] This is called, *Sola Christus,* Christ Alone, which is the very cry of all pardoned souls for justification.[10] Believers who trust in Christ alone to fulfill all the righteous requirements of the Law of God for them, they trust in the one remedy of God's provision for justification. This is to be washed in the blood of Christ's atonement, and it is there, and there alone, that they are covered from God's wrath. Sinners need that

---

[9] 1 Cor. 10:16; Eph. 2:13; Heb. 9:14; 1 Pet. 1:2, 18-19; 1 John 1:7; Rev. 1:5.
[10] This was one of the Five Sola's of the Reformation.

covering, they need that righteousness, because they cannot enter into the judgment of a holy God of unbounded light and truth naked. They cannot appear at the bar of God without a covering; and every sinner who has this covering has it in the same extent, the same power, the same effectual nature and degree; they need the garment of Christ's salvation. All are justified by God through Christ in the exact same manner being born-again believers; there are no levels of justification; they are infinitely atoned for. And if sinners want a covering that will shield them from God's holiness and wrath, they must turn to Christ in faith and repent, and there alone the covering is given to them, exclusively in Jesus Christ who is typified in the mercy seat of the ark.[11] These have, "washed their robes and made them white in the blood of the Lamb," (Rev. 7:14).[12]

Jesus came to fulfill the Moral Law and uphold all things that the believer in him by faith could not do. In the context of Christ being the Light of the world, the Truth of the world, he confirms his mission and work. "Think not that I am come to destroy the Law, or the prophets: I am not come to destroy, but to fulfil. For verily I say unto you, Till heaven and earth pass, one jot or one tittle shall in no wise pass from the Law, till all be

---

[11] "And thou shalt put the mercy seat above upon the ark; and in the ark thou shalt put the testimony that I shall give thee. And there I will meet with thee, and I will commune with thee from above the mercy seat," (Exod. 25:21-22).

[12] We covered this thought in considering faith and repentance in the last chapter.

fulfilled." When is this? When he dies on the cross? No. When he resurrects? No. When he goes to heaven to intercede? No. ...*till heaven and earth pass* ... when is that? At the end. "Whosoever therefore shall break one of these least commandments, and shall teach men so, he shall be called the least in the kingdom of heaven: but whosoever shall do and teach them, the same shall be called great in the kingdom of heaven," (Matt. 5:17-19). Jesus says the church ought to be teaching commandments until the end? Yes. Teaching people to obey commandments to the end? Yes. If ministers neglect teaching the commandments of God to the end, they are least in the kingdom? Yes. Christ alone has justified the believer, washed them by his blood and sent them over to the Law to keep his commands. His cross, his death, his work, his atonement, fulfills all righteousness and satisfies God's desire for perfection in righteousness, for justification. Make a careful note of this important difference. If anyone mixes together anything with the blood of Christ, like trying to satisfy God by their own works, or their own obedience for *justification*, for personal righteous standing before God, it will not wash or cleanse them. Mix Christ's work with a person's works to be justified, and God will never accept it; those people are lost. Why? Christ ushers people into his kingdom by his atonement, and sovereign work of the Spirit in changing them into new men. What can they do for justification before God, to be just in his sight, to be perfect in his sight, to fulfill the

Law in his sight? Nothing: the Moral Law attests to their need to be perfect, to love God and others. They cannot make any legal performance of some sort, though they are required by the Law to be *perfect.* There are no works of merit for them to do because of their fallenness. It is by Christ alone, by God's Mediator alone, that people are saved through being washed by Christ's blood, the blood of the everlasting covenant, because he fulfilled the Law for them for their justification.

What is the effect of Christ justifying sinners? Focus on this, Christ dies, so that believers now may have genuine and sincere penitent faith in him to love God, and love their neighbor; sanctification then *begins.* Love God, love your neighbor, love Christ, love your brethren, these things are intimately conjoined, and always go together. They cannot be separated; sanctification is the work of God's free grace, where men are renewed in the whole man after the image of God, and are enabled more and more to die to sin, and live righteously; this is how the Confession speaks. This is the foundation of action for reformation. How can a person ever strive in reformation of life without being told what to strive for or what to do? And understand, saying, "love God," is very *general,* but it comprises certain truths not explicitly explained in this passage by Christ, but pointing the listener to the Law of God, which is very particular to exercise themselves in for holy purposes.

The generality of Christ's statement, points to the particulars of the acts of love in the Law. The Law tells them what to do to love God, and without the Law they cannot love God. Christ requires the complete reformation of the whole man in light of his Law of love, both by him in his mystical body, which he purchased with his own blood, and with one another, to love one another. That's why he doesn't just say love God and love your neighbor; he says that people are to do this with the entirety of their being - *all*. People cannot love God, and they cannot love their neighbor and they cannot do anything that tends to that end without the blood of Christ washing them so they can, then, do both; their initial faith, repentance and justification leads to their course of sanctification; and their sanctification will then demonstrate their initial faith, repentance and justification. Loving God and loving one's neighbor is to perform the Law in light of Christ's loving power in them, and to be assured of that loving power as they see those works accomplished. It is only accomplished by the Spirit which he liberally gives them; having all things for life and godliness, being able to do all things in Christ who strengthens them to do all things; it is never merely theoretical. When Christ changes a sinner to a saint, that saint knows they could never have fulfilled what God desired on their own, and they know this. They know they have no power to reform their life on their own. But once Christ saves them, and gives them all the privileges of the everlasting covenant through the Spirit, he then takes those saints by the hand and leads them back to the Law to keep it because they *can* now do it; to frame their whole life by it, which all the Bible hangs on these ten commands, this one command to love God and love your neighbor.

The Moral Law is fulfilled for their justification. It is used now for their sanctification. It is *now* very helpful for them, for their reformation.

If a person says "Well, we are not under the Law any longer", they are mistaking the first use of the Law for earning justification and eternal life with the third use of the Law that are still part of the Christian's duty *to be holy*. Christ saves men in order to justify them so that he can lead them back to the Law in order to keep it for sanctifying purposes, to wash them, to sanctify them, to conform them; to make them more holy. The Law has not been repealed or revoked; how could God's character ever be repealed or revoked? It has been fulfilled in Christ so that the righteous requirements no longer remain damning for those under the blood of the atonement. There is no more condemnation for those born-again. In Christ's work, the Holy Spirit applies his death and resurrection, and his present priestly intercession to all his children so that they may be accepted as a result of the reward that Christ has been given by the Father. He sees the travail of his soul in them, and now he prepares them for the wedding banquet; how are they prepared?

Born again Christians have the seal of the invitation to the wedding supper of the Lamb stamped on their soul, but now, he makes them more beautiful until they attend the wedding banquet. He makes them more holy each day, preparing them for the feast. People say they are not under the Law and that the Law has no recourse now for them. That's Antinomian rubbish! It is Anti-Christian. *Antichrist.* Can believers lie now? Can they lust and fornicate now? Can they hate? Can they covet? Can they worship idols? Can they be indifferent to worship of the Father? Can they disregard any of King Jesus' commands? No. Why? Because God's Law stands, and Christ says, love God and love your neighbor, the two tables of the Law showing evidence of one's conversion. God requires his people to reflect his glory as Christians. Christ worked to give them that privilege, and commands his people to pray to that end that they would hallow the Father's name; it's the very first petition in the Lord's Prayer to be holy. *What?* He gives everyone a carnal free pass so they can fulfill their fleshly desires with no consequences because they have a card in their wallet that says "I believed on October 8 on such and such a date?" Rubbish! Jesus teaches that the Christian believer is to love God and love their neighbor – how I ask you? They are to fulfill their duty before God, now led back to the Moral Law by the hand of the Spirit who leads them to do it; remember Samuel Bolton said it frames their whole life, and John Calvin said it leads them by the Spirit to holiness to rejoice in what God has done for them.

Remember, the Lord Jesus Christ the righteous King has not only published his promises but given his people precepts and commandments. He proposes comforts to fallen sinners (promises of grace) to establish their confidence, and he imposes duties (Laws) which require their performance (sanctification). In some places the Moral Law of God is called *the Law of Christ;* the Antinomian does not like that. "Bear ye one another's burdens, and so fulfil the Law of Christ," (Gal. 6:2). To bear one another's burdens is the second table of the Law *to love one another;* bear one another's burdens; fulfill the Law of Christ!

The Moral Law is the Law of Christ. Every time the Son speaks, he communicates the heart of God to his people. Every time in every place, Old Testament or New Testament, it is the Son speaking as the Word of God, except for the Father who commands people to hear his Son speaking, twice, at his baptism and his transfiguration, and a few times in the Psalms and prophets that refer to God enthroning the Christ, as well as at creation.[13] What does the Savior do in the Sermon on the Mount and the Sermon on the Plain but expound the precepts, and presses their practice of the Law on his disciples? And when they, by the Spirit, engage to keep the Law for holy purposes, they find their inability of perfect observance staring back. And what does this do

---

[13] Gen. 1:26; Psalm 2:7, 110:1; Matthew 3:17, 17:5; Mark 1:11, 9:7.

but drive them to Christ for comfort in his promises. And then Christ sends his faithful believers *back* to the Law, as a rule still to guide them in the course of their life. They are by a sincere striving and pressing into the kingdom all their days to observe the King's precepts. Matthew 22 is a very simple Scripture to grasp, but monumental in its scope when it is understood and placed in its rightful context. Love God, love your neighbor, seems simple. Which is why Jesus says, "And why call ye me, Lord, Lord, and do not the things which I say?" (Luke 6:46). Christian obedience is not merely by profession, but by exercise, by practical reformation.

The famous puritan George Gifford in his work on faith and election, teaches in 4 sermons how faith is exercised, and how assurance is experienced in the exercising of one's faith;[14] assurance, what an important topic, to be *assured* of salvation; to *know*. What does he teach first? Most would guess election; I'm elect, now let me consider how I am elect, and what I believe about things to determine my personal election. No, he teaches faith first because he's listening to Peter (2 Peter 1 as his main text) explain how to make one's calling and election *sure*. Their election (that which is understood by theory) is proven practically and will enhance assurance if they think about it in the right way. 2 Peter lays out election, Gifford's text, "Wherefore the rather, brethren, give diligence to make your calling and

---

[14] Gifford, George, *Faith, Election and the Believer's Assurance*, (Crossville, TN: Puritan Publications, 2020).

election sure: for if ye do these things, ye shall never fall:" (2 Peter 1:10). How? Through faith, in which you rejoice, precious faith exercised, in loving God, receiving the end of your faith which is the salvation of your soul, wherefore, gird up the loins of your mind, as obedient children, be holy as he is holy, being built up into a spiritual house, and finally in 2:9, "ye are chosen." Election is argued as a result of *practice* by Peter.

The Reformed Christian church often today has it so backwards because they love considering theory rather than practice! The phrase the frozen chosen is not given by accident, it's given to the Reformed Church because they have their theology backwards as it relates to sanctification. The Moral Law brings the believer back to Christ because of their failure in keeping it to reform them. Then Christ, again, must bring them back to the Law, and deliver his people over to it again, not to its condemning power, but its directing and guiding power as a rule of holiness, as a rule of reformation. The young preacher Andrew Gray said, "A Christian's whole life must be a sweet and constant travelling between Christ and the Law."[15]

How does the Christian life feel as it is worked out? You press into the kingdom, then, epic fail. So you go to Christ, receive pardon and help, seek the Spirit, press into the kingdom again, be filled with the Spirit, strive daily in his power and then epic fail. You then go

---

[15] Gray, Andrew, *Great Precious Promises,* (Edinburgh: George Swintown and James Glen, 1669), 187–188.

to Christ, receive pardon and help, strive again, press, walk, seek, search, look, take heed, pray, read, ... grow ... strive not to get into heaven by works, but a life showing forth holiness and reformation of life because of a love to God. Why do you do this though you epically fail all the time? "If ye love me, keep my commandments," (John 14:15). "How Lord?" you ask. Next verse, "And I will pray the Father, and he shall give you another Comforter, that he may abide with you for ever; Even the Spirit of truth;" (John 14:16-17).

Christ requires the complete reformation of the whole man in light of his Law of love (action), and this will be a pressing and striving until the day of one's death or if Christ returns and does not tarry, in the power of the Spirit who persuades one to the truth of what the Son says in his word.

Again we pause here, and let's turn to an application of this, before we get to consider the heart, soul and mind in the next chapter, for, a *profession* of love to God and Christ is not enough, for this is what Antinomians do. You ask, "What do you mean by that?" God will not ask you on judgment day if you merely spoke the words, "I believe in Christ, I love God, and I love my neighbor, so accept me as a Christian. Let me in..." He will not ask you that. He knows that already one way or the other. He knows your heart, and can peer into it. He knows its depths better than you do. Christ alleviates this idea for us when he says, the greatest commandment is one of action, it is *agape*, love, to God, not merely by way of profession in speech, but in exercise; to exercise one's self before the face of God in the Law of God. Consider, by example, "love to your neighbor" cannot be accomplished in speech, it is impossible overall, it is not merely an intention, it is done in resolute exercise. That means the Moral Law cannot be *applied* merely by *attesting* to it. It can only be applied by exercising it. We have not yet talked about obedience in that regard in relation to Christ's words. But consider, almost every time Jesus talks about real faith, being faithful, being true, being thankful, being converted, being saved, being delivered, it revolves around the exercise of *love to God* in keeping the Law of God. Consequently, on which hang all the Law and prophets; the whole Scripture explains what this means.

There are three levels of understanding coming from Jesus. Level 1 is the teaching of the whole bible. Level 2 is the teaching of the Ten Commandments, on which the whole bible hangs. Level 3 is the greatest command to love God and your neighbor which comprises a summary of the Ten Commandments, on which the whole bible hangs, which is not only professed but exercised. "My mother and my brethren are these which hear the word of God, and do it," (Luke 8:21), they do not merely profess it. In Luke 6 Jesus says, "But I say unto you which hear," ... all kinds of particulars are given in that chapter on the life of the one who follows God, in the sermon on the plain; what does he say to them which hear? I give you the verbs in this passage, "love ... do good ... bless ... pray ... offer ... give." (Luke 6:27-30). These are all words of *action*.

You see, your profession to serve and love God and to be a member of a church, and to confess Christ as the Lord, is not enough even to get into a church. Churches allow believers to get into the external administration of the church by profession; but not by profession alone. Covenanting in the church, joining a church, is housed upon and in *obedience* to the word of God, and it carries with it the discipline of the church and the ordained elders who oversee that discipline. Consider, "And when Saul had come to Jerusalem, he tried to join the disciples; but they were all afraid of him, and did not believe that he was a disciple," (Acts 9:26). You see ... not by profession alone. "I'm a Christian let me in," Saul said. They said "no" to him ... *prove* you are. "You mean, I don't get to do what I want to do in regards to Christ's church? I am not in control?" No, you must prove it by your life; which is the very reason why Christ gave the keys of the kingdom to the elders to allow men in and shut men out of the church (see Matthew 16 and 18); because if men do not prove answerable to their profession, they are disciplined.

Is it not then relevant, for those seeking ordination in a church to be an elder, they are considered in both their doctrine and practice; and in 1 Timothy 3 and Titus 1 the emphasis is in practice? How do they *live?* What is their *family dynamic like?* How is there home a little church? "For if a man know not how to rule his own house, how shall he take care of the church of God?" (1 Tim. 3:5), for those to lead must do as they require others to do according to the Law of God, and love to God. Or this example, "Obey those who rule over you, and be submissive, for they watch out for your souls, as those who must give account. Let them do so with joy and not with grief, for that would be unprofitable for you," (Heb. 13:17). *Obey* means, to be persuaded and to comply (not profess), and the phrase "be submissive" is better translated as "do not resist them." What? You must, "do," and not merely profess? That's why there are keys to the kingdom, and church discipline; because it is not merely about profession. When the life of a covenanter in a church does not match up with their profession, they are disciplined; for the Lord loves those he chastises; he sanctifies them further in action to live answerably to their profession.

The objection comes, "Scripture says, "That if thou shalt confess with thy mouth the Lord Jesus, and shalt believe in thine heart that God hath raised him from the dead, thou shalt be saved," (Rom. 10:9). Or, "For God so loved the world, that he gave his only begotten Son, that whosoever believeth in him should not perish, but have everlasting life," (John 3:16). This says nothing about practice does it? These refer to justification, not sanctification. There is no *belief* without the *do?* Jesus and Paul were not Antinomians. Profession without reformation of life is nothing. Is that the argument people want to give? That's an epic fail. Belief and profession are joined in sincere Christians to those that love the Lord Jesus sincerely. "If any man love not the Lord Jesus Christ, let him be Anathema Maranatha," (1 Cor. 16:22), *i.e.* damned when the Lord comes. "Love not the Lord Jesus Christ?" What is it for you to love? Is it only to speak vocally with words ... or is love an action word? Love God and love your neighbor are impossible without action.

All attempts at reformation of your own life before God and in the presence of other people, is impossible without fulfilling the mandate of love in action. This is why Jesus likens saints and sinners by way of horticulture. "For a good tree bringeth not forth corrupt fruit; neither doth a corrupt tree bringeth forth good fruit. For every tree is known by his own fruit," (Luke 6:43-44). Is he really serious? Good trees don't produce bad fruit? Antinomians will say that every tree is known merely by its profession, a profession of grace. No, profession immediately leads into action. We start with profession, but Jesus said they are known by their *fruit*, because even trees can be deceptive professors. Horticulture again, "And when he saw a fig tree in the way, he came to it, and found nothing thereon, but leaves only, and said unto it, Let no fruit grow on thee henceforward for ever. And presently the fig tree withered away," (Matt. 21:19). He went to see its fruit and it had none and was deceptive in its profession because a fig tree of that kind with those leaves should have had fruit on it based on the time of year; but it was filled with leaves, and no fruit; it was a bad tree. Christ's vengeance is always hanging over the heads of hypocrites because their profession does not match their reformation, their life is not answerable to their profession; so he cursed the deceptive tree. They have no reformation, *they can't have any,* because they have no spiritual motive and habit in them, because they have no Spirit of Christ motioning them to do such things, to bear fruit.

Consider, how will you be judged? Will you be judged by only professing something? Even the devil can say, "Jesus is Lord," and be right. "Even so faith, if it hath not works, is dead, being alone. Yea, a man may say, Thou hast faith, and I have works: shew me thy faith without thy works, and I will shew thee my faith by my works. Thou believest that there is one God; thou doest well: the devils also believe, and tremble." (James 2:17-19). "... faith without works is dead also." (James 2:26). It is interesting that the Apostle James places dead faith, useless faith, false faith, hypocritical faith, counterfeit faith in the position of a mere profession without godly works; and likens it to the belief that demons have. No reformation, no growth, no fruit, means *no salvation.* What does Jesus say to this idea at the judgment? "When the Son of man shall come in his glory, and all the holy angels with him, then shall he sit upon the throne of his glory: ... Then shall the King say unto them on his right hand, Come, ye blessed of my Father, inherit the kingdom prepared for you from the foundation of the world: For I was an hungered, and [you professed to know me] ye gave me meat: I was thirsty, [and you professed to love me] and ye gave me drink: I was a stranger, and ye took me in: Naked, and ye clothed me: I was sick, and ye visited me: I was in prison, and ye came unto me. Then shall the righteous answer him, saying, Lord, when saw we thee an hungered, and fed thee? or thirsty, and gave thee drink? When saw we thee a stranger, and took thee in? or naked, and clothed thee? Or when saw we thee sick, or in prison, and came unto thee? And the King [judgment at the King's feet] shall answer and say unto them, Verily I say unto you, In as much as ye have done it unto one of the least of these my brethren, ye have done it unto me." (Matt. 25:31-46). Not by mere profession, but judged according to one's works before the King, according to the Law of the King's land. If there is going to be a reformation of your life and a reformation of the church (we talk so often of revival), it requires more than a profession of love to God and to love one another. "I'm a Christian," requires action; *it requires you to prove it.* You cannot just confess Christ as Lord and then *not do.* In light of being justified, this is why James connects justification with works in the sight of men. Abraham is the example where he was justified in the sight of men by his works, his profession was not alone. As the saying goes, we believe by faith alone, but not by a faith that is alone. That is a hallmark trait and characteristic of all those who love God and love their neighbor. It comprises the whole of the Law and prophets; it comprises the whole of Scripture.

Your obedience is a requirement for your salvation. Antinomians hate those kinds of statements. They want to sing, "Free from the Law, O blessed condition, I can sin all I want and still have remission." Obedience is a requirement for salvation; and I am at this point painting that statement with broad strokes. Loving God is a fulfillment of the Law, it is part of salvation, one cannot be saved and not love God, and loving God is a good work. *The 1647 Westminster Confession of Faith* 16:2 says, "These good works, done in obedience to God's commandments, are the fruits and evidences of a true and lively faith." They, that is, all Christians, are required "to be diligent in stirring up the grace of God that is in them." Good works do not earn you salvation, they are the light behind your salvation to others, and to yourself, to cultivate assurance; they are part of your walk. Why does the Confession teach the bible in that way? There are three parts to showing forth your salvation, or assurance of salvation that God regularly employs for you in your spiritual walk. Three things that help you know you are saved, that demonstrate your conversion while you live in the world. Do you know them? They could certainly be summed up in love God and love your neighbor, but what does that practically mean and how does that cultivate your assurance of salvation, to even know if holiness is even going on in you by the Spirit. Jesus was purposefully summarizing in his statements, to cover everything here in Matthew 22. There is far more in his explanation, and it is why he explained how that is done through his continued ministry. But regardless of the particulars at this point, do you know the signposts well to help you know you are saved? Three scriptural points are assuring signposts to your salvation and continued reformation making your calling and election sure. Those who truly believe in the Lord Jesus, and love him in sincerity, endeavoring to walk in all good conscience before him, may in this life be certainly assured that they are in a state of grace, and may rejoice in the hope of the glory of God, which hope shall never make them ashamed, as the Confession says. What is the answer to this: that you believe in election? Is that the answer? No, because the bible does not lay out assurance theoretically. It never says, "prove out your election first." It always says *show me your faith*, and *that* will assure you of your election; it will make your calling and election sure. That's Paul's argument in the first 7 chapters of Romans, into 8 and 9. That's James in 1-2, and John in 1 John, and Peter in 2 Peter, and well, all of Jesus' teachings. Consider these 3 things.

The Confession, 18:2, says, Assurance "is ... an infallible assurance of faith, founded upon the divine truth of the promises of salvation, the inward evidence of those graces unto which these promises are made, the testimony of the Spirit of adoption witnessing with our spirits that we are the children of God." In 18:3, "in the right use of ordinary means, attain thereunto. ... And therefore it is the duty of everyone to give all diligence to make his calling and election sure; that thereby his heart may be enlarged in peace and joy in the Holy Ghost, in love and thankfulness to God, and in strength and cheerfulness in the duties of obedience, the proper fruits of this assurance: so far is it from inclining men to looseness."

So, we have three scriptural points. [1] The divine truth of the promises of salvation that you believe in the bible as true. Profession or confession based on the truth of the word; that means you must know something; you have to know what the Gospel teaches. [2] The inward evidence of those graces to which these promises are made through the testimony of the Spirit of adoption witnessing with our spirits that we are the children of God. The work of the Spirit, when you read the bible, attests to those truths that they are true for us personally when we read them. You read Matthew 22, and say, "That's true of me," when you read it. See here what Jesus says, what Paul says, what Isaiah says, what Samuel said, these are true for me personally as I read them. But ... then ... how is it proven? [3] The Spirit's work in us concerning the duties of obedience, the proper fruits of this profession in strength and cheerfulness to God and men. The Bible says it, I believe it because the Spirit gives me "warm fuzzy feelings" about it in my heart concerning me personally, and ... I live it out where there is no question about it because I see it in my life and others see it in my life. Without good works in your life there is no reformation of life, no sanctification, no growth, no degrees of faith. Be keen to listen to this point: without these, there is no love to God or love to men; this is Jesus' point; it's not about talk. Without loving God and loving your neighbor the Christian walk is impossible; that is to say, without the Ten Commandments, there is no Christian walk. Without these there is no loving God with all the heart, soul and mind. It is never, at any time, a mere profession or adherence to the theory of election, which Antinomians love. We are required to do more than the devils do; the Antinomians don't require that. And these three important gateways to assurance are extrapolated from Scripture and are in the church's confession. They use the very words of Scripture to define them.

But let's keep it simple: the Bible says it, I believe it because the Spirit gives me warm fuzzy feelings about it in my heart, and ... I live it out where there is no question about it because I see it in my life and others see it in my life.

Love to God and love to your neighbor is the cornerstone of reformation in your life and in the church, it's never only about confession. Imagine if every Christian loved God and loved their neighbor in action, even in just the right sense of the words themselves, not even to the fullest degree, (because that would only happen in heaven). But at least such Christians would be on the road of reformation. What would cure church divisions? What would cure error in the church? What would cure apostacy? What would cure spiritual declension of any kind in its members? What would cure relational difficulties between people? What would cure every malady in the church? Jesus says, the Law and prophets are the cure. Is that not what Jesus said? A right understanding of the Moral Law of God to love God and love your neighbor found in the Law and the prophets upon which the *entirety* of God's character hangs. Is not the New Testament a commentary and explanation of the Law and the Prophets? Is that not what Jesus taught? Is that not what the disciples taught? Is that not what the whole of Scriptures teaches; that is the entire point of the New Testament; explaining the Old Testament? Jesus did not say to the scribe that loving God and loving your neighbor will be soon found (one day found) in the new writings that come after him after he ascends to heaven, written by new disciples. He said the Old Testament is filled with love to God and love to your neighbor, and in the Gospel of Mark he said to the Scribe that in attesting to that answer, the scribe was not far from the kingdom of God; he gave a right answer, but the scribe just didn't have a right heart. These are kingdom truths, for kingdom business, for kingdom people, to glorify the King of the kingdom, which is why Jesus came preaching the kingdom and the Great King.[16]

---

[16] See my work, *The Kingdom of Heaven is Upon You,* for a full discussion of this point.

I think if you, reader, understand what I have been pressing in these last two chapters, you would read your bible in a very different manner. How would you see Jesus' teaching on the greatest directives for obedience before God and to the Christ if you understood that loving God and loving your neighbor was contained in the whole of the Old Testament? Many Christians just want to read the New Testament, but the New Testament is unintelligible without the foundation upon which it sits. Jesus says your greatest command is to love God and love your neighbor and he summarizes the Moral Law of God which is housed in the Law and prophets, the whole Old Testament – how will you fulfill what God requires of you without being familiar with what he says in it, as he said it? How will you fulfill the greatest commandment if the Apostles and their writings in the New Testament are trying to help you understand what is said in Deuteronomy, or Numbers, or Hosea or the Song of Songs or Exodus?

We tend to wonder why the church is not further along in its reformation as we would hope today. It is because the church at large does not understand the fundamental teachings of Jesus Christ in loving God and loving their neighbor. And is that not established in God's word? And is it not two thirds of God's holy word found in the front part of your bible? How will reformation occur when people think that it surrounds putting a Christian bumper sticker on their car, or wearing a Christian t-shirt? Jesus, as with the fig tree, will question them about their fruitful life or lack thereof. He'll make judgments about them:

> "You wear the t-shirt and have the bumper sticker, but I want to know about what that profession does for you. You say you love me. Tell me about your daily devotional life, what is it like, which shows whether you love me or not; how much time do you spend with me? Do you hear my voice when you read my word? Do you experience the work of the Spirit when you hear me speak to you in the bible? Tell me about your good works, which I prepared in advance for you to walk in. Have you found those good works in Judges, Job, Isaiah, Mark, and Jude? Tell me about your exercise of love to me in your endeavor to hallow My Father's name. Tell me about your work to all my brethren in need. Who have you helped, what have you done for them? How have you given of yourself? Where are you looking to find them? On the streets? Out there somewhere? How have you given of my Spirit in you to others that works for the good of my church body and expanded my kingdom? How has my Spirit overflowed from you to them? You wear the shirt, and have the bumper sticker. You have leaves like the fig tree, but I'm looking for the fruit ... past your mere profession."

What will he say to people who are mere professors on judgment day who have no real fruit? He continues:

> "Then shall he say also unto them on the left hand, Depart from me, ye cursed, into everlasting fire, prepared for the devil and his angels: For I was an hungered, [and you didn't do anything]: I was thirsty, [and you didn't do anything]: I was a stranger, [and you didn't do anything]: naked, [and you didn't do anything]: sick, and in prison, [and you didn't do anything]. Then shall they also answer him, saying, Lord, [when did we not do anything]? Then shall he answer them, saying, Verily I say unto you, In as much as ye did it not to one of the least of these, ye did it not to me. And these shall go away into everlasting punishment," (Matt. 25:41-46).

Jesus is saying, I don't want you to talk about it, I want you to do it; do the fundamentals; people are always concerned in the church about growing the church in numbers, reaching out, telling others about their church, getting it to grow, without being concerned with their own families, and their own devotional life first, without a walk answerable to their Christian confession in the fundamentals of loving God first; for loving God comes before loving one's neighbor. Hear what he is saying, mere profession is *never* enough; this is the same, as saying, love God and love your neighbor, because a mere profession is what Antinomians and hypocrites thrive on.

Keeping the commandments of Christ, is loving Christ. Keeping God's commandments is the evidence that you love God, it is the evidence of your election in him; that makes Reformed Christians so uncomfortable because now they have to examine themselves to see if they fail the test, in Paul's words in 2 Cor. 13:5. Would you like to know that you love God, really, truly? Then do what he commands so it is apparent to you, *and* apparent to others. Keep his commandments, obey his precepts. "Is that really, though, what Jesus means?" Do not take my words for it, Jesus says it blatantly, John 14:21, "He that heareth my commandments, and keepeth them, he it is that loveth me." Love in profession is proven and bound by *doing*. "For this is the love of God, that we keep his commandments: and his commandments are not grievous," (1 John 5:3).

The Antinomian is having a heart attack at explanations like this. They don't want to be obliged to do anything as it relates to salvation. They just want their crown of election. But good works and holiness are part of salvation. Where, I ask you, where are the commandments of Christ, where is the Law of Christ, where are the commandments of God found? Loving Christ's person, and keeping Christ's commandments go together; Jesus will not allow us to separate them. And does not the Moral Law demonstrate to us what we ought to believe and how we are to love the Lord? Is that not what Jesus said? John comments, "And whatsoever we ask, we receive of him, because we keep his commandments, and do those things that are pleasing in his sight. And this is his commandment, that we should believe on the name of his Son Jesus Christ, and love one another, as he gave us commandment," (1 John 3:22-23). Love God and love your neighbor is the whole of the Law of Christ, and this summary of Exodus 20 and Deut. 5, and is both bound in its profession and action, and yet, explained all through Scripture. We have to pause here, and next we will consider this love with *all* the heart, soul and mind, and how it works out in our life in the next chapter.

Chapter 3:
Reformation of
the Heart, Soul and Mind

"Jesus said unto him, Thou shalt love the Lord thy God with all thy heart, and with all thy soul, and with all thy mind. This is the first and great commandment. And the second is like unto it, Thou shalt love thy neighbour as thyself," (Matt. 22:37-39).

I am obliged to remind you of some points we have covered already. Which is the great commandment in the Law? Jesus affirms that the moral Law, comprised of ten commandments, is set in two tables. Table one concerns the object, the means, the manner and time of worship to God. It concerns loving God. Table two concerns actions in light of the first table, loving God, to love one's neighbor and act in accordance with morality to neighbors. Jesus does not recreate a new Law, but explains, most sublimely, what the moral Law *means*, throughout the Law and the prophets. And all this, to love God and to love one's neighbor, is the whole of the Scriptures teaching. It is the whole reformation of the man to newness of life if it is kept as God requires in love. This is the greatest of those things which God commands of his people. To love him and to love others. Such a love to God and love to one's neighbor is to affect the heart, soul and mind toward godly reformation of life. So, Christ requires the *complete* reformation of the whole man in light of his Law of love.

All we know so far is that Christians are not Antinomian, that sanctification is not justification, that the Law plays a role in the life of the Christian, and that we are to love God with all the heart, soul and mind. But we don't yet know what it *means* to love God except that we know it is not merely saying, "I love God," and, that it has some action related to it.

Jesus says people ought to love God with all the heart, soul and mind. Is Jesus serious about the use of his words? When he says "all" is he serious about *all?* Jesus weds a perfect harmony between man's immaterial side with his material side. A perfect harmony between his flesh and spirit in loving God and loving one's neighbor. Can they do this? Outside of Christ, no; in Christ, yes. Believers being accepted through Christ, their good works, also are accepted in him. God, looking on them in his Son, is pleased to accept and reward that which is sincere, although accompanied with many weaknesses and imperfections.[1] "For if there be first a willing mind, it is accepted according to that a man hath, and not according to that he hath not," (2 Cor. 8:12). The infirmities that accompany the performances of God's children do not spoil their acceptance, but their sincerity covers their infirmities because they are all accepted in Christ. The Christian says, *I love God.* They

---

[1] Gen. 4:4 with Heb. 11:4; Exod. 28:38; Eph. 1:6; 1 Peter 2:5; Job 9:20; Psa. 143:2; Matt. 25:21, 23; 2 Cor 8:12; Heb. 6:10; 13:20-21.

know it to be true as it directs them in the word, the Spirit bearing witness to them in the word, and their good works show it to themselves and others. And in their sincerity, they are covered in Christ's work which makes all their biblical works acceptable to God *as reasonable service*. They love God with all their heart, soul and mind in the sincere attempts at all good duties before God. Their whole being is dedicated to God, and God accepts that in Christ. But where do they find the directives to sincere obedience? How does God tell them they are to love him?

What is the summation of the Ten Commandments? If a person were to summarize the Law of God, what would they say? Carnal men would say in a carnal way of working, rules; a list of works; a means of meriting something before God. Jesus Christ says the summary of the Ten Commandments is in the action of *love;* love to God, love to their neighbor. The duty that Christ presses if one understands the Scriptures "in whole" is to love God with the fullness of one's being. The duty is love, the manner that duty is accomplished is through the comprehensive might or power of the heart, soul and mind.

What is love? According to Scripture, love as Jesus would have understood it, is the result of the inward change of the Spirit, and then an informed affection which impels the person to give entirely of one's self to God and to their neighbor. It involves the inner person, in this way, the heart, soul and mind;

interesting that Christ doesn't say *with the body;* he doesn't need to. In covenant with God love runs both from God's direction to his people, and from his people back to God. Man's love for God includes godly fear, delight, striving towards, seeking, trusting, and a godly walking before him; and includes in it a jealousy for God, and a total commitment to him; they are resolute in this in sincerity. Such a love is God-given, a circumcision of the inner most parts of man from being dead in sin, to loving God, as Jer. 31:33, "I will put my Law in their inward parts, and write it in their hearts; and will be their God, and they shall be my people."

Let's, then, use this definition of love: love is a divinely bestowed fruit of God's Spirit in the innermost part of a pardoned soul, likened to a holy fire, motioned in the affections by which a believer is intensely motivated to pursue God as their Supreme Good. This love affects the heart, the soul and the mind; it has to because it would not be able to function without all those parts. It must be an action, exercised from a divine sight or spiritual persuasion of the character and will of God from a new heart and new man given by God. The one who has a divine sight of the Lord, as he has so made himself known in the word, is to have a magnetic attraction to him as that which is the best of beings. And then they do all for his glory and live for his purposes by his will alone.

How does a person know if they love God in this way of a holy fire, intensely motivated to pursue God as their Supreme Good? The one loving, if it is a love that is sincere, exercises a divine love to God according to his commandments. If a person does not have a divine love to God and to Jesus Christ, he is not sincere and does not exercise what God requires of them. He is in a very terrible situation and will be accursed at the judgment, when the Lord returns, as not doing what Christ has instructed of them, or doing it hypocritically. All those who do not love God are still in their sins. His heart is carnal, his soul is perverse, his mind is blind; in fact, all his faculties and affections are corrupt if he has not been made new. The lack of this is that which God complains of; that they draw near to him with their mouth (body), and honor him with their lips (profession with the body), but their hearts were far from him, (Isa. 29:13; Eze. 33); there is no sincere action. But if he does have a sincere love to God and to Christ, it will be, first, with *all* his being. God is not interested in parts or halves (something we will consider in chapter 4); he does not save that way, and does not want his people to act in that way. Christ in the text demonstrates that it is the whole man that is to love God, in its entirety. All his parts in all their divinely given power. The Spirit of God does not change a man in part, but in whole.

As a born-again man was once totally depraved, the Spirit gives him a total new birth and he is totally, and radically, transformed in every faculty and affection; in every part, transformed by grace in heart, soul and mind, and the body will follow. If it is a sincere love, it is loving God back for who he is and what he has done in Christ. Believers love God for God's *loveliness*.[2] Believers love God for God's saving work. If it is a sincere love, it must be a love that is of full Spirit-power. Believers must love God with all their might. Where do they get such a might? They must love him as much as they are able, and count all things, next to him, as something to be hated. "If any man come to me, and hate not his father, and mother, and wife, and children, and brethren, and sisters, yea, and his own life also, he cannot be my disciple. And whosoever doth not bear his cross, and come after me, cannot be my disciple." (Luke 14:26-27). They are never able to love God as fully and completely as God deserves from *their* own power, and so all things *in relation* to that love to God, must take second place. *Love to God* must be above all other things: above possessions, family, spouse, children, work, any things of worldly value. They are empowered by the Spirit of the most high God to love God, and their sincere love is showered in the blood of Christ which makes their sincerity acceptable to God in its entirety.

If it is sincere love, it must be constant, like a kindled fire that continues to be stoked with fuel to burn hotter. Christians would like it to be constant, and would like it to be continued and stoked fully, yet they deal with remaining sin and that causes their love to wax and wane (Romans 7). It burns for God, Christ, holiness and looks there as its ultimate end, but it is not

---

[2] Psa. 27:4, 45:11, 50:1-2, 90:17; Isa. 4:2, 28:5, 33:17; Zech. 9:17.

perfect; it may be raging, or it may be smoking flax. They hear his command, and at times can be dejected because it is saddening to them not to live the way they would like, what they think all of their heart, soul and mind means. But they see the good of God in all his leading and they desire to obey him more and more.

Christ says, love to God with all the heart, soul and mind is the command, it is the whole of the Bible, it is what the whole bible hangs on. Augustine thought that loving God with the heart meant with all the thoughts. Other church fathers included the understanding and the will; that there are various theological ideas around it. Joshua 22:5 says, "Moses the servant of the Lord charged you, to love the Lord your God with all your heart." The heart, soul and mind overlap. The exercise of the will, the place of all thoughts, emotions and feelings. The combination of the mind choosing and heart feeling. The center and seat of spiritual life where the soul or mind, as it is the fountain and seat of the thoughts, passions, desires, appetites, affections, purposes, *etc.*, work and extend. The very way of thinking and then feeling, to love God, is to love him with the understanding and then to feel something about it. Doesn't this require knowing? And this in turn requires the application of knowledge, and the right application of knowledge is called *wisdom.*

There are whole books of the bible dedicated as wisdom literature, to show a man his path to love God. Loving God is not merely a feeling, it is an informed feeling which turns into a holy action, fueled by the word, motioned by the Spirit who is given to every born-again believer. It is the material and immaterial parts of a born-again man working in sincerity.

The soul is the innermost part, the immaterial part, of a living being, a living soul, the seat of all the feelings, desires, and affections. Exod. 21:23, "Thou shalt give life for life;" which translates from the Hebrew, "soul for soul." It is the *life* of a man. One might say, "but did not Jesus say that we are to love God with the heart, soul and mind, and isn't that a repetition then? Don't all these mean somewhat the same thing?" Most assuredly. All these terms overlap. They are saying, in many ways, the same thing from different angles; which is why the repetition is a literary exclamation as a point of reference. All of these intertwine and wrap around one another. If one were to take a basic makeup of man, he is a physical and spiritual being; material and immaterial. These, the heart, soul and mind, comprise the immaterial faculties that cause the physical being to move and live. The heart, soul and mind, the immaterial part, make the material part work and cannot exist as a whole man or whole woman, without it. Whatever the heart does, the body, then, will follow; the same with the mind, and the same with the soul. Christ is saying, the whole bible teaches, that living souls who love God, love God with their whole being sincerely. All the heart, all the soul and all the mind with all their strength, as Mark interprets it adding in the dimension of *power* taken from

Deuteronomy. The point Jesus is making is this, loving God *is not in parts,* nor *only with a certain part.*

Ask any person and see what they think is the most important possession they have while they are alive, and they will tell you their life; and a life is made up of the whole man. Jesus says that a life that loves God, loves him without reservation; the whole man loves him. Loving God is not partial, and loving God is to be done without interruption. Everything a born-again person does, he does for God's glory. There is no part left out, and no task left out that is not part of that love to him. What is it to sin but to interrupt the love the believer has for God? The scribe in Mark, compliment's Christ's answer and says, "And to love him with all the heart, and with all the understanding, and with all the soul, and with all the strength, and to love his neighbour as himself, is more than all whole burnt offerings and sacrifices," (Mark 12:33). It's more than all the ceremonies of the ceremonial Law; and it is. It's more than the blood on the altar; and it is. It's more than going through the motions; and it is. It is more than just doing things for the sake of doing things in the body, there is a sincere motive behind the doing in the heart, soul and mind. Love to God is not annexed or attached to the ceremonial Law, *per se.* Love to God is not annexed to the judicial Law, *per se.* Love to God is directly connected with the morality of the actions of the Law, those things that so demonstrate the character of God in the commands, that they shine in holiness for those that are able to harness them by the Spirit.[3] For only Spirit-filled believers can love God with all their heart, soul and mind, and every action they do in sincerity is accepted by God as with all the heart, soul and mind because it is accomplished in the work of Christ, and soaked in his blood. Only Pharisees see this command as impossible; which is why the Confession uses this very important line, God, "is pleased to accept and reward that which is sincere."[4] One would think that loving God with all the heart is one thing, with the mind is another thing, and with the soul is another thing. It is a very simple point Jesus is making, not to confuse people or make word games, but he is emphasizing the whole man; the entirety of man's redeemed humanity, both material and immaterial is what is in view.

If the heart, soul and mind are dedicated to God, the body will follow along; the body is the vehicle which these other parts are able to love God in the entirety of their redeemed humanity. How will a man demonstrate a biblical reformation of their life, but by a whole desire to be informed and to be exercised in the holiness of God, for the glory of Christ? They are to love God with all the heart, soul and mind, all the time, in every place, for the best of reasons. And this love will do a believer no good, unless it is linked and connected to the Christ

---

[3] Make note, that Old Testament saints who loved God desired to do God's will. Even the ceremonial and judicial laws would have been kept rightly out of a sincere love to God first, and to one's neighbor.

[4] *1647 Westminster Confession of Faith* 16:6.

whom they love. Because until love centers on him as the Supreme good and object, the love goes nowhere and cannot be exercised properly for his glory. Divine love centers on God, on Christ, and is exercised for the glory of God and the good of the man by the Spirit.

Love of this kind is very much associated with possession. Someone might ask, "What do you mean by this, "possession?"" I'm going to trick you here, listen closely: Jesus did not say love God with all your heart, soul and mind. He did *not* say that; so, one might ask, "But then, what did he say? I'm reading it here in my Bible in Matthew 22, these verses of 37-39, and I see here he says *all your heart, soul and mind*." No, that's not what he said, go a bit slower, and consider the phrase that speaks to one's *possession*. Jesus said, Love the Lord thy God, with all ... your heart, soul, and mind. That little Greek word "sou" makes a mountain of difference; *Thy God. Your God. Possession.*

The Bible is filled with possessive statements of this kind concerning God and the believer. Moses, "The Lord is my strength and song, and he is become my salvation: he is my God," (Exod. 15:2). Ruth, "thy people shall be my people, and thy God my God," (Ruth 1:16). The Psalmist, "Thou art my God," (Psa. 140:6). Jonah, "O Lord my God," (Jonah 2:6). Thomas said to the Christ, "My Lord and my God," (John 20:28). The Christian prays, "Our Father" by possession, in Aramaic, "Abba." If men are not sensible of divine glory, and their eyes are not open, they will not see this God, and will never possess him while they are blind, because they possess what they love, and they know what they possess, and they love what is theirs. Possession of the Christ and his saving work, *justification*, will insist without reservation a reflex act of love to God in heart, soul and mind, and the body will follow in its *sanctification*. And make note, that Jesus did not include the body, only because all things are not yet final, and those in heaven, who do not have bodies, love God with all their heart, soul and mind. They are awaiting the day when they can apply this wonderful work of heart, soul and mind, in the context of a glorified body forever.

But how do Christians now love? Is this a circular statement that Jesus makes? Love God with all your heart, soul and mind. But how? With all your heart, soul and mind. No, no, *but how*. How might I love him? What do I do? give me a list. Make me some notes. Give me some direction. What informs me to love God? What is it that all the Law and the prophets teach?

The Law and the prophets teach you to love God with all your heart, soul and mind; it sounds circular doesn't it? "I understand the saying of the words, but what is the *substance* of what motives me to love? Where do I find it? What informs my mind and affections to love him?" one may ask. It is found in that blessed place of his most holy words, the Ten Commandments. The Ten Commandments? Yes. God's Ten Commandments are the rule and practice of the Christian, and informs the Christian how to love God with all their heart, soul and mind. "I don't see how that could be," one might say. "I have liberty, not bondage to the Law," they think. "The liberty of a Christian does not lie in exemption from service, but *in* service; surely that man is yet in bondage who does not judge service as his liberty."[5] "As free, and not using your liberty for a cloke of maliciousness, but as the servants of God," (1 Peter 2:16); freedom to serve; freedom in Christ to love God with all the heart, soul and mind.

The knowledge of God is set down in Laws, commandments, precepts, about the great King who graciously saves and then commands those he saves by the grace of Law. These laws concern the knowledge of God, which are the foundation of a believer's love to God. The Ten Commandments that order the life of believers in the exercise of their love to God, that frame their whole life, either concern the demonstration of their love; or the preservation of them in the love of God. They must show their love to God, and are in them kept in the love of God. In all this, the commandments, and their explanation, their commentary, their unfolding, are their instructions. What is it to love God? It is to love God with all the heart, soul and mind, and this is taught in the ten commandments; so Christians are beckoned by the Son to God *to go to the ten commandments and see what they teach;* but people don't like to go there because they find them too simplistic in their explanation and say that cannot be regulated by just

---

[5] Samuel Bolton, *True Bounds of Christian Freedom*, 350.

those simple statements (but they would be exceedingly shallow to think that).

Is there anything that the commandments do not teach for life and godliness? One may say, well, the commandments really don't teach the Regulative Principle of worship; and we have to look elsewhere in the bible to find that. That God alone determines the manner sinners are to approach him is not found there. What? This is the substance of the entire first table of the Law. The object, the means, the manner and the time of worship. It is regulated by God's word. One may say, the commandments really don't deal with how parents are to teach their children, as the Apostle explains, not to exasperate their children, or provoke them to wrath, in Eph. 6:1. What? What is it to understand the relationship between inferiors and superiors in the 5th commandment? Honor your father and mother assumes the honor of the father and mother to the children, or the honor of the inferior to superiors, and the honor of superiors to inferiors. And what does *that* mean? One may say, but wait, the commandments don't deal with how rich a person should be, or wealth, as the Lord teaches us in the New Testament in Luke 16 about our relationship with unrighteous mammon. The eighth commandment requires the lawful procuring and furthering of our wealth and outward estate of both ourselves and others. The command, "Thou shalt not steal," has annexed to it, forbidding whatever may unjustly hinder our own or our neighbor's wealth or outward estate, and all things attached to that. One might say, but wait, the commandments don't teach divine contentment; how content a person should be in their life as a Christian. What? The duties required in the tenth commandment on coveting, teach a full contentment with our own condition, and such a charitable frame of the whole soul toward our neighbor, as that all our inward motions and affections touching him, tend to, and further all that good which is his; and forbidden in this are any discontentment with our own estate; envying and grieving at the good of our neighbor, together with all inordinate motions and affections to anything that is his.

The one studying the commands will come to find they teach *comprehensibly,* even *in an infinite manner,* the will of God for *all* life and godliness. And most Christians have never taken the time to study them, because they think, "they are no longer under the Law." There is nothing that is not contained in ten words of God that lacks the direction or instruction of one to love God with all their heart, soul, and mind.[6] Is it a wonder then, why the catechisms of the church, really deal with only three areas of teaching? Are you aware of this? A third of the teaching is theological teaching on the basics of the Christian faith; who is God, who is Christ, what did Christ do, what did God create, what happens when people die. A third is on prayer;

---

[6] See my work, *The Ten Commandments in the Life of the Christian,* for an overview of the teaching of the Ten Commandments.

"Lord teach us to pray," as it is found in the Lord's Prayer. And then, a third is on the Ten Commandments; that is what the catechisms teach, and for good reason.

Jesus says that to love God, one must love God's Ten Commandments, or they will not know how to love God with all the heart, soul and mind, and they will never grow in grace, and be further conformed to Christ's image. Can a person lawfully look for a revival of their life, a reformation of their life, without looking to God's commands? I tell you, Jesus says, *it is impossible.* And again, one wonders why the church today, with all their money, and all their reach, and all their ministries, are spiritual *dwarfs* compared to the church of history; it is because they do not know the Law of God and do not really serve the great King, and do not know what it means to love God with all their heart, soul and mind; they excuse themselves from it because they think it is unattainable.

The means to exercise love to God toward godly Reformation is Christ's command. In referring to Christians, Reformation will not take place, without a knowledge of love to God. If that is true, then no reform can *ever* take place outside of the Moral Law.[7] Reformation will not take place without God's Ten Commandments, without his instructions for life, for loving God; consider the *implications* of that. True love

---

[7] This assumes that you understand that the Moral Law, the Ten commandments, cover the entirety of the Christian walk (which they do).

of God and Christ hangs on the Law, and hangs on the prophets, and hangs on the Apostles, and hangs on the letters of the New Testament and all of them direct one to the same thing. Love God and love your neighbor is the *whole* of the Law. (Is this all Christ said? Did he not expound it?) How versed are believers in this? Christians are often versed in sinning against it even in ignorance, but what about in upholding it? "If ye love me, keep my commandments," (John 14:15). Are his commandments new? Are they different? "He that hath my commandments, and keepeth them, he it is that loveth me: and he that loveth me shall be loved of my Father, and I will love him, and will manifest myself to him," (John 14:21). "And hereby we do know that we know him, if we keep his commandments," (1 John 2:3). "He that saith, I know him, and keepeth not his commandments, is a liar, and the truth is not in him," (1 John 2:4). "For this is the love of God, that we keep his commandments: and his commandments are not grievous," (1 John 5:3). "And this is love, that we walk after his commandments. This is the commandment, That, as ye have heard from the beginning, ye should walk in it," (2 John 1:6). "...here are they that keep the commandments of God, and the faith of Jesus," (Rev. 14:12). What? Faith, Christ, commandments? "And the dragon was wroth with the woman, and went to make war with the remnant of her seed, which keep the commandments of God, and have the testimony of Jesus Christ," (Rev. 12:17). What? Testimony and commandments? "Brethren, I write no new commandment unto you, but an old commandment which ye had from the beginning. The old commandment is the word which ye have heard from the beginning," (1 John 2:7). "And now I beseech thee, lady, not as though I wrote a new commandment unto thee, but that which we had from the beginning, that we love one another," (2 John 1:5). And what is it that we love one another, but that the Ten Commandments are summarized in love God and love your neighbor? This is the basic teaching of the Bible.

The Holy Commandments are the means to help believers to love God, and understand his love to them (but this is a study in and of itself to see this in his commands). It's how the Son of God spoke to his redeemed people in the beginning of giving them directions to guide them to heaven, "I am the Lord thy God, which have brought thee out of the land of Egypt, out of the house of bondage," (Exod. 20:2). This is as if God said, "I saved you, and redeemed you graciously, now, listen to me, I am the great King, the Great God, to direct your steps, for I will lead you to green pastures and still waters where you may feed and drink." Scripture not only unfolds the work of his love by the Christ, but also binds his people to love him, by his commands; preachers want to talk about Jesus only as Savior but very little as the Great King. His Laws exhort them to this love, but also produces it in them by this same word, accompanying the preaching of the word with the efficacy of his Holy Spirit, and they concur. I think it has happened to all Christians, where they had the experience, that after hearing the word, the divine sparks of love are kindled in their hearts, and that having that excitement kindled, they were further intensified with his love and their love for him; some movement of the Spirit in them that pressed them with an overwhelming sense of the Spirit's work on and in them and gave them an informed feeling of happiness. What is the word but some explanation of the mind of Christ, some use of God's holy Law applied to them for their good? You find the two disciples in Emmaus, after Christ had vanished, said, "Did not our hearts *burn* within us, when he spake unto us on the way, and preached the Scriptures?" And what Scriptures were these? "And beginning at Moses and all the prophets, he expounded unto them in all the scriptures the things concerning himself," (Luke 24:27). What is it that the Law and the prophets hang on and cause men to burn within themselves? The two tables of the Law. Love God and love your neighbor is what he expounds; everything can be reduced to this. When the Law of God is received into the hearts of born-again hearers, it heats them up and kindles love, and from there reformation will come forth; they will both *know and grow*. There will be a change of life, and reform of the church, in love to Christ, because his commandments are not burdensome.

One will object, Jesus gave us new commandments, "A new commandment I give unto you,

That ye love one another; as I have loved you, that ye also love one another," (John 13:34). Thomas Manton said, "How could he say so, since it was as old as the moral Law, or the Law of nature? New, because it is excellent, as a new song among the Hebrews is an excellent song; or rather, new, because solemnly and specially renewed by him, and commended to their care. New things and laws are much esteemed and prized; so let this my new commandment, let it be highly in esteem and regard."[8] Do men highly esteem and regard the Law of God? Sadly, even among popular preachers, the church today at large is Antinomian.

Reformation will not take place without the Spirit's work through God's Law in the believer. Men do not keep the Law to be justified, but they certainly keep the Law to be sanctified. Reformation in love to God is an effect of the Spirit of sanctification, which God only gives to his children. Any grace which may further a believer's reformation should make them willing toward such a change. This Spirit must accompany them, that they may fervently desire this; how many today fervently desire the Law of God? Such a Spirit works in believers to the very end that they may not will something in vain, and without fruit. Philippians 2:13, "It is God which bringeth forth in us with efficacy, both the will and the deed, according to his good pleasure." What is his good pleasure but for believers to love him with all their heart,

---

[8] Manton, Thomas, *The Complete Works of Thomas Manton*, Vol. 10, (London: James Nisbet & Co., 1872), 325.

soul and mind? Shall I ask again, and what is the *substance* of that? God does not force people, like rolling a stone, to move. He desires the love of a believer to be fanned and enflamed for him. The Spirit pushes and prods and directs, and what will the believer do? Will they follow?

"But I don't find Jesus in the Law," one might say. "I am the Lord thy God, which have brought thee out of the land of Egypt, out of the house of bondage," (Exod. 20:2). That is Jesus talking; who do you think is talking? Countless books have been written expounding this wonderful preface to the commands. It is the communication of the Son of God from the mountain to the people. The Word, the eternal Logos, is speaking to them. The eternal Word is expounding the character of God, the Law of Christ. The shadow of the type, deliverance from Egypt, from sin, to come into the place of God's worship. It is the Son speaking, and he looks for the believer's love to be reciprocal for delivering them from bondage of sin. I am the Lord thy God who has saved you. That is because God is the Lord, and our God, and Redeemer, therefore, we are bound to keep all his commandments; that is his directive, with our whole being, with every part, in sincerity in him. The Christian is not to reserve for himself some part not given to God; they were bought with a price; therefore, *glorify God in your body and in your spirit which are God's*. It is eminently Christ centered; they are justified by Christ to serve the Great King in holiness, with their whole being.

It is the greatest commandment to love God with all the heart, soul and mind, with every part, and to its fullest degree; this is what they strive in and to. Such gives way to love others, to love neighbors, as one loves themself.

How do you love Jesus with all your heart, soul and mind? You say with the excuse attached to it, "I don't, I can't." Why do you say that? Jesus' words don't mean that you can't, it just means that you won't; and you need to fix that. You say, "that's easier said than done." True. But not mere something you say, but exercising holiness in sincerity, and you *can* do that. Christians must stop making the, "I can't do it" excuse. Are you not Spirit empowered and led?

Do you love God like his people loved him in Scripture? "There was a man in the land of Uz, whose name was Job; and that man was perfect and upright, and one that feared God, and eschewed evil," (Job 1:1). Do you fear God and eschew evil? "Noah was a just man and perfect in his generations, and Noah walked with God," (Gen. 6:9). Are you a just man or women? Do you walk with God? "For I know him, that he will command his children and his household after him, and they shall keep the way of the Lord, to do justice and judgment;" (Gen. 18:19). Do you do justice and judgment? "...my servant David, who kept my commandments, and who followed me with all his heart, to do that only which was right in mine eyes;" (1 Kings 14:8). Do you keep all his commandments? Did David sin? If he did then you are not thinking about loving God with all your heart in the right way, because you are thinking that to love him with all the heart, soul and mind is to be *without* sin, and David was a sinner, as was Noah, Job, Abraham. Look at Asa, "And Asa did that which was right in the eyes of the Lord, as did David his father," (1 Kings 15:11). Do you do what is right in God's eyes? Josiah, "And he did that which was right in the sight of the Lord, and walked in all the way of David his father, and turned not aside to the right hand or to the left," (2 Kings 22:2). Do you not turn aside to the right or left? Zacharias and Elizabeth, "And they were both righteous before God, walking in all the commandments and ordinances of the Lord blameless," (Luke 1:6). Are you blameless, walking righteously? Mary, "thou that art highly favoured, the Lord is with thee: blessed art thou among women," (Luke 1:28). Are you highly favored? "Simeon ... was just and devout" (Luke 2:25). Are you just and devout? "To the end he may stablish your hearts unblameable in holiness before God, even our Father, at the coming of our Lord Jesus Christ with all his saints," (1 Thess. 3:13). Do you deject or despair over words like these? If you are a believer you shouldn't, for here is the clincher. "He hath not beheld iniquity in Jacob, neither hath he seen perverseness in Israel," (Num. 23:21), which is why the Scriptures can speak this way about believers and their walk. Why does God *see no iniquity* in them, in all of them, regarding them as righteous, and blameless? It is all because of Christ. Because God considers them as they are in Christ. Because he considers them as they are going to be in Christ as a perfect bride.

Hebrews 11 (the HALL OF FAITH) names no sin because God sees those people in their end, just like he sees you in your end as you walk before him blameless and upright, loving God with all the heart, soul and mind, so as to never impute condemnation by the Law. Just, devout, blameless, righteous, one with a heart after God, walking in holiness ... if you are a believer in Jesus, this is your description too. "The Lord beholds not iniquity in Jacob, neither sees perverseness in Israel," (Num. 23:21); and as Christopher Love said, "but this is not, as the Antinomians try to make it say, as if God did not see sin in his people, and is never displeased with their sins; but the meaning is, that God sees not sin in his people so as eternally to punish it."[9] God will not punish you as born again, for he punished Christ for you already. Nor does he want you dejected to say, "I can't do it," for, "shall we go on sinning that grace may abound?" And what is the answer but, "certainly not."

God sees you as a believer, out from under the Law. There is no condemnation in this for you if you are born again. As it pertains to justification, you are just, devout, blameless, righteous, one with a heart after God. And if you are, then are you delighting to walk in sincere holiness? God will say the same things about you as he did Asa, or David or Job.

---

[9] Love, Christopher, *Grace: The Truth and Growth and Different Degrees*, (London: E.G., 1652), 62.

Jesus directs you this very day, love him with all your heart, soul and mind. Whatever your love is to him, is the power that sustains a godly reformation in your life. Is there a balance between how much you love God and how much reformation occurs in your life and how much of the Law of God you take in and know? Yes. All things considered, and presuming one is both converted and the Spirit is willing to set that heart, mind and soul on fire, what is the balance? How are you to motivate yourself to be better in religion this week than last week, knowing you are still walking in that course of remaining sin? It is the same as asking how are you *motivated* to love God. What could motivate you to love Christ more?

As you are considered in him as perfectly righteous, so you are to consider his directives as those things to comply with. And yet, there are benefits for you in this, past the benefit of being justified. There are two benefits of holiness that you should know, 1) transformation now, and, 2) the capacity of your happiness later. To know him more is to be like him more now, and this is a great benefit. How do you know him more? "By his word," you say. And what do all the word of God hang on for you to know him more to love him more, to love him with all your heart, soul and mind to be like Job, Asa and David? Is it not his kingly commandments? Can you find a more excellent object for exercising your love than Jesus' word and will to you in your sanctification of the whole man? His commandments make you holy, and show you how holiness should look, to fear God and eschew evil, to walk uprightly, to be holy; and is he not ravished with holiness in his church, "one eye and one chain," as the Song of Song says? He sanctifies all your sanctification. One eye and one chain will *ravish* him. Whatever sanctifying powers he sees in you, he is ravished with as a believer because it is him working in you – I find no Scripture to give us excuses to this. If you are holy, and you heed his commands, you will be like him, transformed and conformed into his image; imagine that.

Jesus is the greatest and best of beings. Can you love lesser things, and not the greatest good? Can you love lesser things and not heed the greatest commandment? Can you love the greatest commandment of loving him in sincerity, and for reformation of life, but yet, without the instruction he provides in doing so? Maybe you don't like holiness so much because the commandments are not suitable to you. You want freedom and liberty to choose your own dealing and your own path, your own way and your own worship, your own religion, your own rules. You don't want to be told to do things. Why would you desire to remain in ignorance to the very tools that God gives you to reform, that beautify you? He does not give you a thousand, or even a hundred commandments. He gives you one; love God without reservation, and the second is like it, to love your neighbor. So many people weary themselves trying to find the gate of eternal life, and yet they miss it because they miss the pointer and directive of the Christ to his one commandment to love God more than all. They miss seeing what the Law actually does, and how Christ leads them to it as believers. They throw it away, and look for a republication of that Law in the New Testament somewhere thinking that unless Christ said it all over again that it doesn't count, as if he did not set it down already before. In the commandments is found the beauty of the Christ, if they are understood, and they show forth the way of salvation, all things that pertain to life and godliness, and these commands beautify you as a believer, however little or much you engage in. He has supplied you with his commands, and has made them new to you by giving them to you in one command, one easy command really, for his commandments are not burdensome.

But so many do not think they are very satisfying because they look to them as a list of legalistic rules to be saved, rather than a means to love God with all the heart, soul and mind. There is a great difference between legalism and obedience in this. Legalism is trying to earn one's justification by keeping the Law, obedience is doing what the great King commands, which is a means of rejoicing in him for what he has done in you, for he sees every act of your sincere obedience to him as blameless, and upright, and righteous. Are these commandments not the most delightful commandments ever given in light of that? Are his words not a delight to you in this?

The love of Christ is the best love you can attain, and the Christ himself is the object that should have your greatest love. What then? Such instructions are very sweet to the spouse, but you must know them. They are only hard and burdensome to those who do not have the Spirit, or do not know them. Without Jesus and his Spirit aiding you to make those commandments a delight, and not burdensome, such an attempt to love God with all the heart, soul and mind becomes bitter and hard, "it is too big and I can't do it," the distressed soul thinks. Those in hell hate God's Law, for they have found it eminently bitter, will not do it, will never do it, and do not love God. They do not love Christ, or his words, and his commandments they cannot stand them because they are those Scriptural lines that condemn them at every turn. They grieve and groan under these torments of thought, that they have done poorly, and neglect the Christ, and his word, and his Laws, and his commandments, and statues and precepts, and do not nor ever have loved him. All the commandments that God has given them, they find *tedious*.

I hope you don't find them tedious. Do you find it a burden to pray? "Thou shalt have no other gods before me." Do you find it a burden to hear or read the word of God? "Thou shalt not take the name of the Lord thy God in vain." The Law can be difficult when you have a very small love to Jesus; that is true. Because love to God makes hard things easy, and heavy labor light.

Love God with all your heart, soul, and mind is not so hard because the Spirit makes it easy for you, because Jesus made it easy for you. Does not Christ deserve that kingly love, and as he has so instructed you to love him according to his commands? Will you deny Jesus what is due to him in loving him in this way?

You should say:

"I know I cannot keep these Laws perfectly, but I will try. I will try by the Spirit of Christ, to fulfill the Law of Christ. Though I cannot do as much as I would like to do, or as best as I would do it, Christ will not lose my love. I will love him with all my heart, soul and mind, as I can, and as the Spirit has given me the power to do all things for Christ, and I can do all things for Christ; he is no liar. And I will strive for it. I will be informed in it, and will be reformed by it. For I know that Christ requires my complete reformation in light of his Law of love. He shall have my heart, soul and mind in love to him."

Thomas Doolittle said, "Is there any love so universally necessary as love to Jesus? One man loves one thing, and a second another, and a third another. But there is no necessity that all men should love any one thing except for Jesus, and things pertaining to our having and enjoying him. Love to Jesus is absolutely necessary for poor and rich, for great and small, for noble and lowborn, for learned and unlearned, for slave and free."[10] And where shall we find the means to love him so? What will we mine out of God's word that will reform us and that thoroughly, while at the same time showing our unbounded love to Christ? Christ requires the complete reformation of your whole man in light of his Law of love, and you may, by his Spirit, love him as such.

A second motive to loving God with all the heart, soul and mind, is the promise of reward he gives you, the capacity of happiness later. I think a great many Christians are not motivated by this, and should very much be. Some Scriptures to this point will be helpful: "...but to him that soweth righteousness shall be a sure reward," (Prov. 11:18). "Rejoice, and be exceeding glad: for great is your reward in heaven," (Matt. 5:12). "...and thy Father which seeth in secret shall reward thee openly," (Matt. 6:6). "He that receiveth a prophet in the name of a prophet shall receive a prophet's reward; and he that receiveth a righteous man in the name of a righteous man shall receive a righteous man's reward," (Matt. 10:41). "...and every man shall receive his own reward according to his own labour," (1 Cor. 3:8). "For God is not unrighteous to forget your work and labour of love," (Heb. 6:10). "Knowing that of the Lord ye shall receive the reward of the inheritance: for ye serve the Lord Christ," (Col. 3:24).

---

[10] https://www.apuritansmind.com/the-christian-walk/motives-to-love-jesus-by-thomas-doolittle/

In opposition to this thought: "Alexander the coppersmith did me much evil: the Lord reward him according to his works," (2 Tim. 4:14). One of the most famous: "Now if any man build upon this foundation gold, silver, precious stones, wood, hay, stubble; Every man's work shall be made manifest: for the day shall declare it, because it shall be revealed by fire; and the fire shall try every man's work of what sort it is. If any man's work abide which he hath built thereupon, he shall receive a reward. If any man's work shall be burned, he shall suffer loss: but he himself shall be saved; yet so as by fire," (1 Cor. 3:12-15).

What you do now matters for eternity. Should Christians love God simply for what he is, and what he has done, with all their heart, soul and mind? Yes. But isn't it a most gracious and wonderful thing that God even gives *rewards* to his people for their labors in holiness? Good works are not rewarded for *justification*. Good works are rewarded in *sanctification.* God is not obliged to do this, but freely does this. The saint's good works shall all be rewarded in heaven. If we give a cup of cold water to a disciple in the name of a disciple (Matt. 10:42), we shall not lose our reward. Those that do fewer good works will have a less reward, and those that do more good works will have a greater reward. 2 Cor. 9:6, "He that sows sparingly shall reap sparingly; and he that sows bountifully shall reap also bountifully." The Antinomian says, you mean to say that if I do nothing, and this fellow over here does ten things his capacity for happiness in heaven is greater than mine?" Yes. "That's not fair," he says. It has nothing to do with fairness. God is able, of his determination, to give rewards for works; both good and evil and to whatever degree those works reap. Listen to Edwards, "We are justified and saved entirely by Christ's righteousness. We are delivered from sin and hell and we have bestowed on us eternal life through Christ alone; but what is the capacity of the saint in the happiness of eternal life? This is a very good question. Jonathan Edwards defined this helpfully, Eternal life is "happiness that is perfect or that fills the capacity of the creature.""[11] Does eternal life, then, mean that every capacity is the same, and how are these rewards by God applicable to making heaven more heavenly? Christ's work doesn't impede the saints from being rewarded. It doesn't impede the saints having various capacities and various degrees of happiness in heaven. Christ did not purchase a particular *degree* of happiness for all of you. If that were true, and if he did, all Christians would be exactly the same in their sanctification, and that instantaneously at conversion. In general, he purchased perfect happiness for all of you as justified believers. Everyone's capacity in heaven shall be filled perfectly, and it will be perfect happiness. But, to what degree of

---

[11] Edwards, Jonathan, "None Are Saved by Their Own Righteousness," in Sermons and Discourses, 1723–1729, ed. Harry S. Stout and Kenneth P. Minkema, vol. 14, The Works of Jonathan Edwards (New Haven; London: Yale University Press, 1997), 337–338.

happiness, that is of different degrees. Every saint will be cast into the ocean of Christ's happiness, and every saint will be filled to his greatest degree. Christ saved them in that way. But how large is the container of that happiness for each saint, this is determined right now; in this life, in your works, which you shall be rewarded for, will determine it. It is determined in the Spirit's work in sanctification concurring in you as a believer while you live here and uphold Christ's commands, or not. "If any man's work abide which he hath built thereupon, he shall receive a reward," the apostle says. This should be a grand motivation to you as a believer. To be more like Christ now, most assuredly. To be rewarded more by him at the judgment, that is a *wonder*. The more you do in loving God with all your heart, soul and mind, by his statues and Laws, in Christ, by the Spirit, the more he will reward your capacity for happiness in heaven; Christians are not drones; God has determined it otherwise; you are not some stone rolled up a hill that God rolls, without your help; he does not save you without you, he does not sanctify you without you. Is it no wonder Scripture says things like this: "The righteous also shall hold on his way, and he that hath clean hands shall be stronger and stronger," (Job 17:9). "But the path of the just is as the shining light, that shineth more and more unto the perfect day," (Prov. 4:18). "Strive to enter in," (Luke 13:24). "...and every man presseth into it," (Luke 16:16). "...the kingdom of heaven suffereth violence, and the violent take it by force,"

(Matt. 11:12). "So run," (1 Cor. 9:24). "...let us run ... the race that is set before us," (Heb. 12:1). Why is Scripture replete with language like this? Very simply, to love God has rewards with it, "And, behold, I come quickly; and my reward is with me, to give every man according as his work shall be," (Rev. 22:12), and all this is directly related and attached to Christ's requirement of the complete reformation of your whole life according to his Law of love, in that one command, which rests in those ten commands, on which the whole Scripture hangs. That it is not a burden to love God, but that even in this, you are rewarded for doing so.

Now, the opposite to this love of God, is hypocrisy, which we will consider in the next chapter as a conclusion to our study.

Chapter 4:
Serving God in Halves

"But Jehu took no heed to walk in the Law of the Lord God of Israel with all his heart: for he departed not from the sins of Jeroboam, which made Israel to sin," (2 Kings 10:31).

Jehu "walked not" in the Law of God with all his heart, the scripture says, and the proof is given, because he had a reservation in *one* point; "he departed not from the sins of Jeroboam," (2 Kings 10:31). Jehu, did many good works, such as destroyed Ahab's house, killed the worshippers of Baal, and many good services. Who was this king?

In following his life in somewhat of a chronological timeline, I will give you the following summarized considerations as taken from Scripture and outlined in *The Lexham Bible Dictionary*[1] that gives an excellent and concise outline of his life:

Jehu, the king of Israel, his name meaning "Jehovah is he," was the son of Jehoshaphat, the son of Nimshi (2 Kings 9:2, 14). He reigned in Samaria for 28 years (841–814 BC) after destroying the Omride Dynasty and establishing his own that lasted four generations (2 Kings 10:30). The biblical account of Jehu's service is

---

[1] See the section under Jehu, King of Israel for a much longer and more detailed account.

found in 2 Kings 9–10. His rise to power was a result of the religious conflict between the prophets of God (led by Elijah and subsequently Elisha) and the followers of Baal, who received political and military support from King Ahab and his wife, Queen Jezebel (1 Kings 18:4, 13). After Elijah defeats the prophets of Baal on Mount Carmel (1 Kings 18:20–46), God instructs him to anoint Jehu as king over Israel (1 Kings 19:16). Jehu served as a captain in the army of Joram, the son of Ahab, and aided in Israel's fight against the Arameans at Ramoth-gilead (2 Kings 8:28–29; 9:5–6). The anointing actually occurs later, conducted by one of the "sons of the prophets" at the guidance of Elisha.

Jehu's rise to power is seen in 2 Kings 9:1–37. Elisha sends one of the sons of the prophets to Ramoth-gilead to designate Jehu as king (2 Kings 9:1–13), as was the case with the anointing of both Saul and David (1 Sam. 10:1, 15:1; 1 Sam. 16:1–13). The prophet instructs Jehu to eradicate the house of Ahab as revenge for the murder of God's prophets (2 Kings 9:7–10) which fulfills a prophecy given by Elijah in 1 Kings 21:20–24. Jehu's fellow soldiers show their allegiance to him, and Jehu begins his military rebellion over King Joram, (2 Kings 9:13–14). Ahab ended the ancient strife between Israel and Judah through the marriage of his daughter to Joram (2 Kings 8:18; 2 Chron. 21:6), this union also created the way for an increased influence of Jezebel. With her influence, the worshippers of Baal increased in prominence, and those who maintained faithful worship to God repeatedly faced persecution (1 Kings 18:4). Although Ahab's military efforts often brought great victories to Israel, (1 Kings 20:13–21, 26–30), his campaigns and building plans put monetary pressure on the nation. For example, in the Battle of Qarqar (853 BC), Ahab employed 2,000 chariots and 10,000 foot soldiers against Assyrian king Shalmaneser III. By the time of Jehu's rebellion, Israel was involved in another conflict—this time with Hazael, king of Aram (2 Kings 8:28–29). Joram, who had been injured in this battle with the Arameans, flees to Jezreel in order to heal from his wounds (2 Kings 8:29, 9:15). When Jehu learns that Ahab's son is within striking distance, he marches to Jezreel. After sending two watchmen to inquire of Jehu's intentions, Joram, accompanied by his nephew (King Ahaziah of Judah), personally greets Jehu (2 Kings 9:17–21). When Joram asks Jehu if he comes in peace, Jehu says that peace is impossible given the spiritual "harlotries" and "witchcrafts" of Joram's mother, Jezebel (2 Kings 9:22). When the king attempts to flee, Jehu kills him with an arrow to the heart, (2 Kings 9:23). Using Naboth's property to dispose of Joram's body, Jehu sees his actions as divine fulfillment of Elijah's prophecy against Ahab.[2] Since Ahaziah, king of Judah, is also a member of Ahab's household (2 Kings 8:18, 26; 2 Chron 21:6), Jehu orders his death too. After assassinating Joram and Ahaziah, Jehu confronts Jezebel. Upon learning of Jehu's arrival, Jezebel paints

---

[2] 1 Kings 21:19; 2 Kings 9:25–26.

her eyes and adorns herself (2 Kings 9:30), preparing to die like a queen. She then addresses Jehu as "Zimri" (2 Kings 9:31), connecting him with another king of Israel who had murdered his predecessor and seized the throne for himself (1 Kings 16:8–20), trying to make him look bad. Jehu asks Jezebel's attendants to cast her out of the palace window, and they do (2 Kings 21:22–23). Jehu tramples Jezebel's body with his horses, and her remains are devoured by dogs in fulfillment of another prophecy by Elijah (1 Kings 21:23; 2 Kings 9:33–37).[3]

Now Jehu Reigns (2 Kings 10:1–32). He continues his destruction against Ahab's household. When he discovers that 70 remaining descendants of Ahab are in Samaria, he writes to the leaders and elders of the city, (2 Kings 10:1). He says that, since Ahab's descendants are in the city with chariots, horses, and weapons, the elders should choose the best soldier from the household of Ahab, set him on the throne, and then send the new king to challenge Jehu in battle, (2 Kings 10:2–3). When the elders receive the letter, they are terrified of what Jehu may do (2 Kings 10:4) and respond by indicating that they have no desire to put anyone else on the throne, (2 Kings 10:5). Jehu then states that, if the leaders are on his side, they will take the heads of Ahab's descendants and bring them to his court at Jezreel, (2 Kings 10:6). The elders assassinate Ahab's sons and

---

[3] Hamme, Joel T., "Jehu, King of Israel," ed. John D. Barry et al., *The Lexham Bible Dictionary,* (Bellingham, WA: Lexham Press, 2016) section under *Jehu.*

bring the heads to Jezreel, placing them in two large piles at the entrance of the king's gate, (2 Kings 10:7–8). This display not only discouraged future rebellion, but also made the inhabitants of Jezreel aware that Samaria, the capital city of the northern kingdom, was under Jehu's control. Jehu also murdered Ahab's men, acquaintances, and priests, (2 Kings 10:11). When 42 relatives of the late king Ahaziah arrive to greet the royal family, Jehu orders them to be executed, even though it is clear that they know nothing of the rebellion, (2 Kings 10:13–14). While these actions may have benefited Jehu's immediate self-interest, they caused the political problems in the country and Jehu was rebuked by God (Hosea 1:4), since these murders fell outside the directions given to Jehu at his anointing (2 Kings 9:6–9). Jehu then encounters Jehonadab, the son of Rechab, who also gives Jehu his support (2 Kings 10:15). Josephus asserted that Jehonadab and Jehu were old friends, and Jehu indicated that he had no intention of allowing any false prophets or priests to live (Josephus, *Antiquities* 9:132–33). By aligning himself with the leader of the Rechabites, Jehu was probably trying to win public support by demonstrating that he also had a "zeal for the Lord" (2 Kings 10:15–16). Once he arrives in Samaria, Jehu kills the remnant of the house of Ahab, ending them (2 Kings 10:17).

Jehu then focuses on eradicating Baal worship. Acting under a lie that he is an ardent follower of Baal, Jehu summons all the prophets, priests, and worshipers of Baal to assemble and offer sacrifices to the deity (2 Kings 10:18)—in fact, he declares that if any Baal follower who does not arrive will be put to death. He intended to kill all those who appear for the sacrifice (2 Kings 10:18–19). When all the worshipers arrive at the house of Baal and offer sacrifices, Jehu orders 80 men to secure the building and ensure that none of the Baal worshipers escape alive (2 Kings 10:24). Jehu's officers then execute the worshipers, burn the sacred pillars in the building, demolish the temple itself, and turn it into a "draught house" or toilet (2 Kings 10:25–27). Jehu's actions demonstrate that Baal worship will no longer be tolerated within the kingdom of Israel.

Now, interestingly, because Jehu followed God's instruction on this, and completely eradicated the house of Ahab, God promises him that his descendants will remain on the throne of Israel for four generations, (2 Kings 10:30). His royal descendants were Jehoahaz, Joash, Jeroboam II, and Zechariah, who served as the final king under Jehu's Dynasty (2 Kings 15:12). Only Omri and Jehu succeeded in establishing dynasties in the northern kingdom that extended beyond the second generation.

However, Jehu did not walk in the "Law" of God and observe it with all his heart (2 Kings 10:31). Even though he fulfills Elijah's prophecies, Jehu does not act with God-honoring motives; his body did much where his heart did not. Instead, he permits the religious practices that were instituted by Jeroboam (including the worship of golden calves in Bethel and Dan) to remain in the land of Israel (1 Kings 12:26–32; 2 Kings 10:29, 31). As a result, God begins to shrink Israel and to allow the country to fall into the hands of Hazael, the king of Aram (2 Kings 10:32–33).[4]

Now, what shall we say of this fellow, and the text at hand? Hypocrites take no heed to walk in the Law of the Lord God with all their heart, soul and mind. Serving God with part of the heart, is serving him half-heartedly, and this is a great sign of hypocrisy.

Where there is a constant heedlesness in duties before God, it is a great sign that one is a hypocrite. Jehu did many great works, but he did it in halves, half-heartedly, which rendered everything he did vain. He took no heed to walk in the Law of the Lord God of Israel with all his heart. To keep, guard, observe, give heed,

---

[4] Extrabiblical references of Jehu are even mentioned as one of the few Israelite kings from the 9th century attested in ancient Near Eastern sources outside the Bible. The Black Obelisk, The Black Obelisk of Shalmaneser III (ca. 825 BC) depicts Jehu coming on his hands and knees before the Assyrian king (ANEP, 122, 291). Shalmaneser states that Jehu gave him a number of items, including "silver, gold, a golden saplu-bowl, a golden vase with pointed bottom, golden tumblers, golden buckets, tin, a staff for a king, and a wooden puruhtu" (ANET, 281). It In the inscription, Shalmaneser reports receiving tribute from "Jehu, the son of Omri." Although Jehu was not from the Omride dynasty, Israel was often known as the "land of Omri" to her neighboring countries (Hobbs, 2 Kings, 116). In addition to the Assyrian inscription, a 9th century Aramaic inscription known as the Tel Dan Stele appears to reference events that the Old Testament attributes to Jehu. In the inscription, an unidentified Aramean king (typically thought to be Hazael, contemporary of Jehu) claims to have killed a king of Israel and a son of the "house of David."

have charge of, watch, to protect; guarding the heart is done in accordance with God's Law *for* the heart.

It is impossible for anyone to be constant in God's service acceptably without watching over their heart and without keeping the Law of the Lord. David says, Psalm 119:112, "I have inclined my heart, to perform thy statutes always." "Keep thy heart with all diligence; for out of it are the issues of life," (Prov. 4:23). It is only a good and honest heart that is able to make a person follow, walk and give heed to God's Law and God's ways, as the Christ shows in the great command to love him with all the heart, soul and mind. In the parable of the sower he says, "But that on the good ground are they, which in an honest and good heart, having heard the word, keep it, and bring forth fruit with patience," (Luke 8:15). Jehu did not have a good ground, or an honest heart, did not look to the word of God, did not keep it, and did not bring forth fruit with patience. He fell away, though he did much for God in covenant. Such a half-hearted attempt at religion made Jehu fall away in the end, notwithstanding all the pleasant confirmations he made of zeal for God, and his truth; at the time, he may have been praised. But Jehu did not take any heed, to walk in the Law of the Lord God of Israel, with *all* his heart. And because he rejected walking according to God's word, it made his heart hungry for other things. Things like embracing Jeroboam's idolatry of worshipping the calf; most likely a political benefit for himself. In the same way it is like Simon Magus who fell

121

even though he had a number of fine shows of religion, even in being in the company of the Apostles, and being baptized. In the end, Jehu showed exactly what he was. It is never how well one thinks they have *begun*, but how they remain *constant*, and certainly how they *end*. Jehu was a mighty reformer, but only of outward reformation, not inward. He did not reform his heart. He had a natural heart in the end. "He took no heed to walk in the Law of the Lord with all his heart," (2 Kings 10:31). Though some of his works seem to be very zealous for God, he was rotten on the inside. The Lord Jesus observes that the Pharisees, "pray, to be seen of men;" and fast, so, "that they may appear to men to fast," (Matt. 23:25); a show on the outside, but painted tombs on the inside.

When Christians resolve to repent and amend their lives, and walk in *goodness* in the light of God's Law, to work their obedience before him already being justified by faith, but being obedient as Christians, they must never reserve to themselves any allowance of any sins. God forbids and severely punishes all sorts of sin. The Christian's resolution must know their duty, and extend that duty and service to God in everything which God has required of them with a whole heart, in sincerity. This religious purpose, or resolution, by the Christian, is what the commandment expressly calls for when they are to love God with *all* their heart, soul and mind, (Luke 10:27). For if they keep a secret reserve for any sin, their heart is given *but by halves to God*, and is not *whole* with him. Jehu did not walk in the Law of God with all his heart, the Scripture says, and the proof is given, because he had a reservation in *one point,* and did not depart from the sins of Jeroboam, (2 Kings 10:31). "David," God says, "followed me with all his heart;" which appears because he did only those things which were right in God's eyes, (1 Kings 14:18). The Psalmist says, universally of all who love God, "They seek the Lord with their whole heart, who do no iniquity," (Psa. 119:2-3). These are high ends indeed, but done in Christ, by the power of the Spirit, where all they bring to God in service is set under Christ's work.

The Law of God is the rule in walking *wholly* and *holy* before God. The promises which man appropriates certainly imposes on him certain duties, and among them the duty to obey the Law of God as a rule of life, but also carry with them the assurance that God will work in him, "both to will and to do."[5] God works his work in them by the Spirit. God works his Law in them by the Spirit. God works all duties in them by his Spirit, yet, they concur in that working to exercise those motions. Believers have the infinite Spirit in them. What do they lack? What can't they do for God?

The Scriptures teach and allow that true faith, and no other, fuels a desire to keep God's commandments. A true, lively, justifying faith, rests only on Christ for justification, only by the imputation of his righteousness on believers. But such a faith never looks

---

[5] Phil. 2:13.

at duty as legalism, nor does it look at obedience as unnecessary. The Moral Law of God as a rule of Christian conversation and sanctification, acknowledges the conformity to it as a duty which God requires of every true believer. Otherwise, people will take *no heed* to walk in the Law of the Lord God of Israel with *all* their heart.

When people profess God, and yet, do not walk in the Law of God with all their heart, soul and mind, the grace of God may be said to be abused and perverted to a wrong end. When professing Christians abuse this grace of God to give profession without exercise of godliness, they have a rest in the mere outward *show* of enjoying that grace, and the benefits of the Gospel, but have no spiritual or lasting fruit. Do they labor for a true and real interest in the benefactor himself, as well as the benefits? These people, who profess to be made free in Christ, think that it is enough to be counted free, an have to do nothing else; but ... this was not what Jehu did, for he did *much*. People even doing less than Jehu did, such people have half a Gospel; but like Jehu many of them have half a heart. In this way there are many people who only care to have a name, or to have the uniform of a Christian soldier because it looks good on the outside. Christ says in Rev. 3:1, these are those who "receive the grace of God in vain," and why? Like Jehu they took no heed to walk in the Law of the Lord with all their heart.

Such half-hearted professors never thrive in godliness, and are as much slaves to sin as ever they were if they think the Christian life is only a mere profession, and nothing more. They abuse God's authority because they do not take heed to walk in the Law of the Lord with all their heart. Such half-heartedness is a great sign of their apostasy. In the, "Antinomian heresy, the sons of Belial evidently do prove in the practice of their Lawless and graceless life, show how this Antinomian fire is, as an enemy to true faith, and the power of religion, so a friend to all other heresies now a foot, especially to popery, serving as a marker for it by breaking down the walls of the city of God."[6] It is *abuse* by people in their *not walking*, for they do not do even as much as hypocritical Jehu did. They abuse the grace of God when they cast off their required obedience to the Law of God as their rule of life. When these people cast off their duty, they think it is because God casts off this duty from being under the Law, or under condemnation by the Law, and because *grace* frees them from sin, *to sin,* so then they are without any need to watch, or take heed, or to work – saved by grace, they think. It is very plain by Paul's explanation that some people would conclude from the doctrine of free justification by Christ, that they might continue in sin, to the end that grace might abound; should men test God in this? That evil might be done, that good might come from it? That there are some even taught this, whom Peter calls seducers, (2 Peter 2:18-19). These people would infer an

---

[6] Burton, Henry, eBook, *The Law and the Gospel Reconciled,* (Coconut Creek, FL: Puritan Publications, 2014) To the Reader.

utter repeal of the Law of God denying that it has any directive, or regulating power over a Christian believer. They misunderstand what is abrogated and what is not. In respect of justification believers expect acceptance from God, not for what they are or what they have done, but by relying on Christ alone.

In respect of condemnation, Christ was made a curse for them. But they are to have a delight in the Law; they are different people now. And in their obedience to it, after they are converted, if it is sincere and not hypocritical, that obedience is accepted through Jesus Christ, and God rewards them for this for their sanctification. As a rule of life, such commands forever continue. Love is the whole of the Law; faith will pass away into sight, and hope will turn to reality in heaven, but love will never fail, and in heaven, as on earth, God's will shall be done into eternity; because love never fails (1 Cor. 13). Jesus says that the greatest commandment, which is a summary of the Law on which the whole Scripture hangs is set on love, which shall never end. The ceremonial Law vanishes, decays, waxes old, is broken down, changed, disannulled, abrogated, which the Scripture testifies is fulfilled in Jesus Christ.[7] But the Moral Law of God, not one iota, not one jot, not one tittle of it shall ever be dropped. The Spirit of God frequently admonishes believers not to reject keeping the Law of God under a pretext of Christian liberty. "For, brethren, ye have been called unto liberty; only use

---

[7] Phil. 2:24-25; Heb. 7:12, 18, 8:13.

not liberty for an occasion to the flesh, but by love serve one another," (Gal. 5:13), as the second table of the Law says. Then, "As free, and not using your liberty for a cloak of maliciousness, but as the servants of God," (1 Peter 2:16), which refers to the first table of the Law. These others, these hypocritical professors, they take no heed to walk in the Law of the Lord God with all their heart. If disobedience to the Law is still a sin in the believer, and it is, its power is not abolished. They then are classified by Christ as law-less. "Many will say to me in that day, Lord, Lord, have we not prophesied in thy name? and in thy name have cast out devils? and in thy name done many wonderful works? And then will I profess unto them, I never knew you: depart from me, ye that work iniquity," (Matt. 7:22-23). This last phrase, "work iniquity" is ἀνομία (anomia) meaning, 1) the condition of being without the Law, because they are either ignorant of it, or because of violating it, and in this way having a contempt and violation of it. Jesus condemns all law-less-ness with *hell*.

Jehu went to hell in 814 BC and he is still there because he was a hypocrite. But as it relates to the professing Christian, serving God half-heartedly is a great sign of hypocrisy. It makes Jehu your spiritual father.

Hypocrisy is opposed to the reality of the work of the Gospel in a man's heart, as opposed to what is real in a man's heart; that is hypocrisy. When a person has an appearance of what they do not really have, hypocrisy lies in a deficiency of the principles that should be in a person *but are not*. They have no real foundation; it is all sinking sand for them. When they pray, hear preaching, and do duties that are appropriate to the will of God, with no real spiritual reality of these things in their own heart, having nothing within but the flickering of natural affections, when they have no clear judgment to discern their own state, in this they are *hypocritical*.

Hypocrisy is like a movie star where a person simply acts out the part; they know that they are not really those things. And such a hypocrisy as this is Jehu's sin, his outward show, his half-heartedness, without any inward change. He wanted to be counted for a strictness and holiness that he did not really have. And yet, in the flesh, hypocrites *do* much. They will hear sermons, and pray and read the bible, and fellowship and such things. But such people take no heed to walk in the Law of the Lord God with all their heart. Such professors see walking with God and a strict adherence to the Law of God as too difficult and dismiss it. King Jesus sees it as obedience if it is in sincerity. They do not see it as a rule of righteousness, sweetened and perfumed with Gospel-grace, to perform personal obedience in the eyes of King Jesus who requires it with all the heart, and commands them to it. The hypocrite misses that obedience to the Law is not legalism; that God will in fact congratulate them if they do well outwardly from an inward principle. Yes, the Law of God has been fulfilled by the Christ, who has removed the curse, but who then gives his people the power, in the Spirit to obey it, they full knowing that Christ's blood pardons all their sinful imperfections of disobedience. They know they are not justified by works through keeping the Law, (that door to heaven is shut, never to be opened to sinners) but by faith, (which is a gift from God to them) laying hold on the righteousness of Christ freely, and looking only to the pure grace of Jesus Christ reckoned to the sinner's account. They are not legalists, they are servants. And those who cast off sincere obedience like Jehu did, are not. And think it through, he was negligent in only *one thing* according to the Scriptures; and that one thing trickled down into numerous sins.

People who want no Sovereign over them, who do things by outward show and by halves alone, such people take no heed to walk in the Law of the Lord God with all their heart. Yet, Christian practice is plainly spoken of in the word of God. It is the evidence of the truth of grace, not only to others, but to one's own consciences. It is a *chief* evidence. Imagine if God simply shouted down from heaven and said, "There is a saint, there is a saint. There is another saint," and pointed them out. But God says, "He that hath my commandments and keepeth them, he it is that loveth me." "If ye love me, keep my commandments," (verse 15). "If a man love me, he will keep my words," (verse 23). And, "He that loveth me not, keepeth not my sayings," (verse 24). "Every branch in me that beareth not fruit, he taketh away; and every branch that beareth fruit, he purgeth," (verse 2).

"Herein is my Father glorified, that ye bear much fruit, so shall ye be my disciples," (verse 8). "Ye are my friends, if ye do whatsoever I command you," (verse 14). "If ye continue in my word, then are ye my disciples indeed," (John 8:31). "Hereby we do know that we know him, if we keep his commandments," (1 John 2:3). "Whoso keepeth his Word, in him verily is the love of God perfected; hereby know we that we are in him," (verse 5). Psalm 15 says, "Who shall abide in thy tabernacle? Who shall dwell in his holy hill? He that walketh uprightly." "Who shall ascend into the hill of the Lord? And who shall stand in thy holy place? He that hath clean hands, and a pure heart," *etc.* (Psa. 24:3–4). "Blessed are the undefiled in the way, who walk in the Law of the Lord," (Psa. 119:1). "Then shall I not be ashamed when I have respect to all thy commandments," (verse 6). That is a few Scriptures on this point. Is it enough?

But hypocrites who look only for an outward show, take no heed to walk in the Law of the Lord God with all their heart. Yet, Jehu had done much, but was very self-deceived, for he did not do all he should have because he had a bad heart. "Little children, let no man deceive you; he that doth righteousness is righteous, even as he is righteous: he that committeth sin is of the devil," (1 John 3:7–8), this is a very bad heart. "He that saith, I know him, and keepeth not his commandments, is a liar, and the truth is not in him," (1 John 2:4). And: "If we say we have fellowship with him, and walk in darkness, we lie, and do not the truth," (1 John 1:6). The hypocrite's heart is as a signpost to their profession. In this way, Spirit-filled works to the Law of God are the highest evidences by which Christians ought to give trial to their sincerity in loving God with all their heart, soul and mind. But hypocrites who look only for an outward show, take no heed to walk in the Law of the Lord God with all their heart. This is truly to be a child of Jehu, and to serve God but half-heartedly.

Make a trial of your own heart. You must make a trial of your heart that you are not like Jehu. Are we conscience of our sin and our obedience, or lack thereof? Surely, we are; conscience is biting for the redeemed. It was not biting for Jehu. A biting conscience is a very good thing. What do we do in light of our beloved sins? Hypocrites, they take no heed to walk in the Law of the Lord God with all their heart, and they serve God by halves; what do *we* do? Jehu seemed to be, in many things, a very zealous and godly kind of person; at least outwardly. But there was one sin he could not leave, and the hypocrisy of his heart was discovered by that one sin, (2 Kings 10:31). "But Jehu took no heed to walk in the Law of the Lord God of Israel with all his heart: for he departed not from the sins of Jeroboam, which made Israel to sin," (2 Kings 10:31). Who made a record of this but the Spirit of Christ? Our hearts are not out of his view. What showed so blatantly was that he did not have an upright heart because he did not cast off the sins of Jeroboam. Why? Maybe he thought it was politically profitable to him in some way? People would like him more if he left that false worship intact. It was a familiar sin; he would not leave it off. Israel was used to it, and to get rid of it, might cost him his kingdom by the disparagement of the people. He was outwardly bound a hypocrite in one thing; and what made him a hypocrite was an unchanged heart (inwardly), in loving that sin more than he loved God. Loving that sin was very great. He was more strongly inclined to that sin, and that sin yielded him more pleasure then other sins did, it was beloved to him. He did not have a conscience which strove against it, and hated it, and desired to cast it off, pushed to grow out of it. He was comfortable in it. He allowed it without striving. You see, hypocrites take no heed to walk in the Law of the Lord God (to strive) with all their heart.

The sincerity of your profession very much depends on the care you have in taking heed to the Law of God from your hearts. This is the case of Jehu, as it is in many professors. So many good things he did; (the Pharisees did *so much*). Jehu was even given a reward by God for his service against the destruction of Ahab's wicked house and Baal worshippers. But, Jehu is forever inscribed in Scripture as a hypocrite. God rejected this man because he did things for selfish reasons, and insincerely, or half-heartedly, as only an outward show. He didn't look to have his heart cleansed; just part of the land cleansed. Any professing person that does not take heed to their heart, that is not careful to order it according to God's Law, is considered a hypocrite. "And they come unto thee as the people cometh, and they sit before thee as my people, and they hear thy words, but they will not do them: for with their mouth they shew much love, but their heart goeth after their covetousness. And, lo, thou art unto them as a very lovely song of one that hath a pleasant voice, and can play well on an instrument: for they hear thy words, but they do them not," (Ezek. 33:31-32). They serve God by halves; outwardly they seem to serve him, but not from the heart; for those who reject the Law of God as a rule and guide, serve God partially, half-heartedly; and show themselves hypocritical at best, and apostates at worst.

Are you fearful of making a trial of your own heart in this way? For you as a Christian, (if you are born again), there are sweet and sure signs of salvation and election; things you love. Following the truth, in sound wisdom and judgment is something you love. Your rebuking of sin inwardly, a poverty of spirit from there, and a mourning is something you love, (Matt. 5:3-4). The beatitudes are not preached by Christ as something to be obtained, but that are *already* obtained by those who *are* such things; they are present in such people. A meekness of spirit, to cast ourselves down at Christ's feet, (Matt. 5:4). A hungering after the righteousness which is in Christ alone, and a price placed on it, with great esteem above all earthly things (Phil. 3:8-9). A thinking on, and a desire to speak of heavenly things. A conflict of the flesh and spirit, and in this, by practice, the power of the Spirit getting the upper hand throughout your life (Rom. 7:23). A sowing to the Spirit, by the use of the means of grace, such as studying the word, prayer, godly meditation, family worship, public worship, and other good works. A of vowing of one's self wholly to the glory of God, and good of our brethren, taking up Christ's two tables of his command to love God. An unreserved resignation of ourselves into God's hands in all things. An expecting of the daily increase of our soul's health, looking forward in hope one day to the body's resurrection and glorification. The forgiving of all people, even our enemies. An acknowledgment of our offences, with a purpose truly to leave them in repentance, with a contrite spirit before God. A delight in God's worship, congregation and saints. A spirit without guile: that is, a happy disposition and purpose always to do well, no matter how many difficulties we encounter.

There are many sure notes of practical works, which give a sign of salvation, in which we do, but we look to our heart, and desire and long after such graces. And we know that in such looking to do good works, all this is still a looking to Christ.

Christ is the answer to all hypocrisy. Christ warns vehemently against hypocrisy. "Ye hypocrites, well did Esaias prophesy of you, saying, This people draweth nigh unto me with their mouth, and honoureth me with their lips; but their heart is far from me. But in vain they do worship me, teaching for doctrines the commandments of men," (Matt. 15:7-9). He connects the commandments of men with hypocrisy because men should be upholding the commandments of God by love to God, not just with the body. "An hypocrite with his mouth destroyeth his neighbour: but through knowledge shall the just be delivered," (Prov. 11:9). The psalmist also expresses more, they seek the Lord with their whole heart, who do no iniquity, "Blessed are they that keep his testimonies, and that seek him with the whole heart. They also do no iniquity: they walk in his ways," (Psa. 119:2-3). Jesus says, "If a man love me, he will keep my words: and my Father will love him, and we will come unto him, and make our abode with him," (John 14:23). Be genuine and sincere in your desire to please him and you will be rewarded for it. "...love ye your enemies, and do good, and lend, hoping for nothing again; and your reward shall be great," (Luke 6:35). The reward for faithfulness in this life, at least one aspect of that, is *greater* responsibilities. The servant whose pound produced ten was not given the lack of responsibility, a paid vacation. He was appointed ruler over ten cities.

Also, don't be myopic, and look at only one instance, one time, one kind of sin in your life; this is what Christians often do. Take your life, and all your works, and consider the things you do overall, rather than in one instance, here and there. That is why the saints are all said to be *faithful.* Consider your *life* collectively. If you have been a Christian for ten years, look over those ten years; what growth do you see? Those who look at their life under a microscope, in the sense that they get very frustrated and will have little rest in Christ, day in and day out, it is because they concentrate on their individual failures instead of having that keen eye that searches out the Spirit's work in them, concurring in them, by them through them throughout their life. Never look at your life with an eye only to *daily* failures, instead of a *life* of holy service. Consider your beginnings, yes, consider your current state, most assuredly, *but end well.* How can you end well but by striving and pressing, and taking the kingdom by violence with absolute zeal? But, consider, that in the narrative, Jehu is noted for *doing many good things*, but is also noted for being a hypocrite in *one* thing, but that one thing was associated with an overarching spiritual problem, which was a wrong heart (an unregenerate heart).

Know that in all your works of loving God with all your heart, soul and mind as a believer, God receives them in Christ, if you are in Christ. Weak works are still accepted in him. He sees no iniquity in Jacob, remember? He will not crush the bruised reed, or quench the wick of the smoking flax if it falls from the lamp. The metaphorical language is powerful in that illustration. Reeds were used in the ancient world as pens. They are used to build boats, and even houses if they are not damaged. If they are damaged, if they are crushed, the only option is to break it and use it for cooking or heating. Every home needed some form of light. Small clay lamps were used and fueled with olive oil. The wicks made from these materials of such lamps hung from a spout at the side of the lamp. As the oil ran out, there was danger that the wick might separate through burning and the flaming end would fall out of the spout and cause a fire. A bowl of water was often placed on the floor under the lamp to prevent it. But the Servant of God, described in Isaiah 42, will not crush the bruised reed, nor will he quench the little flame. He sees David following with his whole heart. He sees holy Job eschewing evil. He sees Samson as faithful. He sees you in both your sincerity and in your walk, both being acceptable to him as you strive and press and take the kingdom by violence if you have a right heart. You know your works are weak, and often tempered in some way by sin and the world, not done as you would like them to be, and Jesus knows this, but he will not *quench* you in it. But bring Christ to everything he commands, and when you are exercising in it, God accepts it. It is true that he has given you a non-negotiable standard by which he will reward all your works. They will be weighed and reward will be given. But nothing for you in Christ is condemnation, though you may suffer loss, and yet be saved. He will not turn a sore eye to you and say, "badly done," at the judgment seat. No, like those in Hebrews 11, he will see and does see what you are in Christ, and what you will be in Christ and regards no iniquity in you. But this does not open a door for you to sin so that grace many abound. It opens up to you the lightness and pleasantness of loving God and tasting of the sweetness of Christ now in this life, to look forward to what it will be like to love God with all the heart, soul and mind in heaven without reservation, forever. Take hold of it now, and taste of it now.

Loving God with all the heart, soul and mind is the sum of all religion. It is the greatest act you can do before the majesty of the great King; it is his greatest commandment. The essence of all holy religion to Christ is to love him back, because he first loved you. That is why the greatest part of true religion before God is to love him with all the affections; the whole being. Love is the sum and substance of all true virtue before God, and dispels hypocrisy in every form. Duties done only by the body without a new heart, are hypocrisy, which is why Jesus did not include the body in his great command. Should this love not be in very great degree in us? Should it not be cultivated as such? Shall we not strive in it? Shall we cast away all excuses against it? Shall we not rest in its pleasantness? Let the exhortation of Christ sit well with you to love God sincerely, and strive for that love in its greatest degree always. Jehu was cast away for having a hypocritical heart. He was cast away regardless of what his body did. His heart did not do it. His zeal was an outside zeal, not an inward zeal. Your heart, must be of a different nature than his. Augustine said, "If God is man's chief good, it clearly follows, since to seek the chief good is to live well, that to live well is nothing else but to love God with all the heart, with all the soul, with all the mind."[8] So, live well, cleave to God alone, serve him, maintain a good purpose, follow his Law, hear his word, see all of Christ's Laws as sweet, and lament all your imperfections with remorse, looking to Christ who gives us both pardon and peace; and so unlike Jehu, you take heed to walk in the Law of the Lord with all your heart to the glory of God, and in this you will fulfill the work of Christ's great commandment in his Law of love.

FINIS

---

[8] Augustine of Hippo, "On the Morals of the Catholic Church," in St. Augustin: The Writings against the Manichaeans and against the Donatists, ed. Philip Schaff, trans. Richard Stothert, vol. 4, A Select Library of the Nicene and Post-Nicene Fathers of the Christian Church, First Series (Buffalo, NY: Christian Literature Company, 1887), 54.

Other Helpful Books Published by Puritan Publications

Consider some of Dr. McMahon's other works:

John 3:16, Second Edition
5 Marks of a Biblical Church
5 Marks of Biblical Commitment to the Visible Body
5 Marks of a Biblical Disciple
5 Marks of Biblical Reformation
5 Marks of Christian Resolve
5 Marks of Devotion to God
Augustine's Calvinism
Christ Commanding His Coronavirus to Covenant Breakers
Eternity Weighed in the Balance
Covenant Theology Made Easy
Historical Theology Made Easy
How to Live Every Day in the End Times
Joseph's Resolve and the Unreasonableness of Sinning Against God
Seeing Christ Clearly
Systematic Theology Made Easy
The Five Principles of the Gospel
The Kingdom of Heaven is Upon You
The Two Wills of God Made Easy
The Reformed Apprentice, (Workbook on Reformed Theology)
The Reformation Made Easy

Also, consider these newly published puritan works:

A Call to Delaying Sinners
by Thomas Doolittle (1632–1707)

A Treatise of the Loves of Christ to His Spouse
by Samuel Bolton, D.D. (1606-1654)

Attending the Lord's Table
by Henry Tozer (1602-1650)

Faith, Election and the Believer's Assurance
by George Gifford (1547-1620)

God is Our Refuge and Our Strength
by George Gipps (n.d.)

Remembering Your Creator
by Matthew Mead (Mead) (1630-1699)

Repentance and Prayer
by Ralph Brownrig (1592–1659)

Resisting the Devil with a Steadfast Faith
by George Gifford (1547-1620)

Taking Hold of Eternal Life in Christ
by George Gifford (1547-1620)

The Believer's Marriage with Christ
by Michael Harrison (1640-1729)

The Blessed God
by Daniel Burgess (1645-1713)

The Cursed Family,
or the Evil of Neglecting Family Prayer
by Thomas Risley (1630–1716)

The Doctrine of Man's Future Eternity
by John Jackson (1600-1648)

The Victorious Christian Soldier in Christ's Army
by Urian Oakes (1631–1681)

Zeal for God's House Quickened
by Oliver Bowles B.D. (1574-1664?)

The Sweetness of Divine Meditation
by William Bridge (1600-1670)